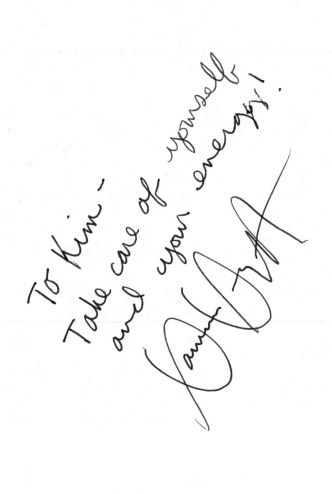

WORKPLACE HEALERS

HEALERS

THE HEALING ART
OF LEADERSHIP

SAMM SMELTZER

DEDICATION

To:

The East Coast Institute of Medical Qigong
Master of Medical Qigong Class of 2021
and our incredible teacher, Ted O'Brien

Chuck Christianson

Karen Greenstein

Diane Mizrahi

Lyle Wilson

Gwen Wong

Thank you for your presence
while I have navigated my healing.

You were each instrumental
in my cultivation and awakening.

Gratitude and love for you always.

CONTENTS

Part Three
The Hawk Shows Us Why We Should Care

Part Four
HR Healer Toolkit

THE EMPLOYER'S PERSPECTIVE

I have worked in the field of education for most of my adult life. Minus a five-and-a-half-year span of time when I first got into HR, my career has been centered around K-12 public education – first as a teacher and later in HR. As a teacher I was always struck by comments from parents and community members indicating their dislike for a new educational program, process, or schedule, because "that's not how we did it when I was in school." This commonplace argument for why change in education, whether on a large or small scale, should not take place is not based on any educational, psychological, or sociological theories or best practices, but rather solely on personal experience and preference. As if merely having "been there and done that" makes one an expert on the topic.

Of course, this happens in other places too, not just in education. I think about spectators at sporting events who used to play that sport themselves – very often they end up "coaching" from the stands or from their living room sofa. And let's not forget the workplace, where supervisors and leaders were once employees too. It's often easy for us to think we know better when we have been through a related experience, but I would argue it is a dangerous habit to get into, especially in the workplace.

I always find it interesting the number of managers and supervisors who believe they know what their employees think, feel, and/or need without ever asking them. They "know" because they were an employee once. Now that's not to say that someone who started at a company as an employee and later became a supervisor can't understand the plight of employees in that company to some degree. But when it is based solely on your own experience, that very self-centered view is rarely accurate due to the complexity of the overall culture and climate of an organization. Times change, industries change, and people change.

What's needed is employee involvement and engagement. And engagement doesn't happen in an organization when its employees, including its management and leadership, need healing. Healing must happen first, then engagement, deep, impactful engagement, can occur.

Healing starts with us as individuals. We can't lead healing and change in our organizations if we are broken, tired, or lacking resiliency. We must attend to ourselves first so we can be in a space where we can then assist others. The workplace is more challenging than ever right now, and HR is perfectly poised to lead the way, but only if we tend to our wellbeing. We know, our bodies know, when we need to heal – the challenge is learning to recognize that intuition, to hear the inner cry for help, and then taking the steps to heal.

What Samm has done in *Workplace Healers* is invaluable for HR practitioners, employers, and employees alike. She has provided an assessable path for HR practitioners to first heal themselves and then assist their organizations in accessing the true organizational needs in order to heal their culture/climate as well.

I have been on my own healing journey both personally and professionally for several years now, and it is truly an ongoing journey. I am blessed to call Samm not only a dear friend, but my spiritual soul sister as well. And so, as a part of my journey I have gotten to work with her on many of the practices and concepts she shares in this book. I have found the principles and tools in *Workplace Healers* to be enlightening, powerful, and impactful for me in my role as an HR practitioner, and I think you'll find the same to be true for yourself.

To heal one must first be healed. So, whether you are looking to just heal yourself, or you are looking for ways to help a handful of employees or the entire organization, this book is a phenomenal resource. Samm's simple to follow, self-paced, thought-provoking exercises, activities, and practices throughout this book will help you as an HR practitioner to not just survive, but rather to thrive, in these challenging times.

—Bobbi Billman
Human Resources Director

The Employee's Perspective

There I was seated on a padded seat in a law office on the top floor of the building. The whole building made me feel uncomfortable and severely underdressed, but it was my annual review so I was meeting the Board President at her office. Despite my nerves, the review went so well that by the end of the conversation she surprised me by offering me the opportunity to become the next Executive Director of my workplace. That meant I would become the next leader of one of the most prominent art centers in town. As a former art kid who constantly heard that it was impossible to get a job in the art field, this was a dream come true… right?

But all the praise and excitement fell flat against my eardrums. I was shaking. If this was a dream come true, why was I hesitating? She was staring back at me waiting for my answer, but I had nothing. This *should* be my next exciting step, and I *had* worked incredibly hard for it.

If this was such a dreamy invitation, then why was it that my office was so often the setting of my nightmares? Why had they just fired one of my closest friends on staff in a humiliating way and with no warning? My body hurt. My social anxiety was off the charts. I could barely stand to attend the mandatory gallery receptions with a smile on my face. I was full to the brim with resentment. The thing was, I was massively burnt out – burnt to a crisp. I thanked the Board President but told her I needed to think about it.

Slowly over the next several hours, it dawned on me that this job was actually making me sick, and the reason for that was much more intangible than I at first assumed.

Initially upon taking the job, I thought I could fix things by streamlining every system I could get my hands on. I thought I could grab the office by the ears and pull it into the modern age – pushing everyone to finally go digital and work on a shared file system. I went well beyond my job description and developed routines and schedules for things that always fell through the cracks. My work there was so effective that I expanded the revenue and reach of my department to new levels nobody thought possible, but I noticed my hard work hadn't even touched the problem that I was actually trying to fix – that thing that was making all of us miserable.

Lying in bed that night, I realized that I didn't have the power or knowledge to fix the organization, regardless of whether I rose to the level of Executive Director. I was finally able to admit that I was in one of those toxic workplaces.

Shortly afterward I started my job search. I felt like an animal desperate to move to higher ground, and though I put my best foot forward, I quickly grew hopeless that I'd find a new job that was any different. In small ways and big, hiring managers continuously communicated to me that as a potential employee, I was worth absolutely nothing.

I heard this over and over through hundreds of hours of jumping through application hoops that resulted in no call-backs. I heard whispers of worthlessness from the company looking for an office manager when they told me I'd have to close my tiny art business while working their low-pay part-time job, stating it would be "too much of a distraction." I heard this in the interview where two managers talked about me as if I wasn't sitting right there in front of them. They were taking bets on whether or not I'd be able to fix the incredible amount of drama present in their current team, and after admitting that I was the only applicant they had for the thirty positions they needed to fill ASAP, they still laughed at me when I asked for more than the meager $10/hour and no benefits they were offering. I was trapped.

This is the plight of the employee who relies on a paycheck to pay the bills. This is the struggle of the hardworking person with no financial safety net waiting behind their every decision. To this kind of employee, our current workplace culture feels abusive and seems to feed off our desperation. To call it suffering is not an understatement or dramatization. This is reality for so many employees just like me.

I was hired at the HRart Center as Samm's Director of Strategy and Operations. Years prior I was one of her Healing Qigong clients, and it was then that I learned about the relief a healing modality can bring to a burnt-out non-profit employee. Despite this powerful experience, I still couldn't imagine how life-changing it would be working for a business that brings those same concepts into its very foundation. The HRart Center is a prime example of what a human-centered business can look like.

To give you a taste, my work schedule is designed to fit around my wellbeing and art practice, because the HRart Center understands that those two elements in my life have the power to make me the best employee I can be. Though I work about half as many hours as I used to, I've never been more productive. My bills are paid, I have health insurance, and though work is still work, I get excited to start every time I clock in. I'm slowly healing every day.

It's clear to me now that my former workplace needed (and undoubtedly still needs) a Workplace Healer. A Workplace Healer could walk into that space, read the collective energy, and expertly unravel the toxic workplace culture, which was that intangible broken part that I couldn't fix. It's not just that we need to heal a place like this because we want to increase ROI or decrease turnover, but most importantly, this sort of deep healing work will have massive effects on anyone who interacts with that organization. The ripple effects spread and improve everyone's overall quality of life, and what could be more important than that?

Employees *need* Workplace Healers. The people who work above you, your peers, and especially the people you manage need you to heal yourself and learn to heal others. Your people are the ones who need you to step onto the path of becoming a Workplace Healer.

—Stephanie Holmes
Director of Strategy and Operations

Introduction
The Unsaid

It was Spring 2018 and I was invited to speak on facilitating culture change. The conference committee challenged me to fill my session with tangible takeaways. You know stuff that people could implement almost immediately. I debated on doing research to jazz it up with recommendations that people may have never seen or heard, but instead I decided to keep it simple and honest. I showcased the one tool that I had utilized time and time again.

The tool was a SWOT analysis which I'm sure is familiar to you. It is a common business tool that is typically taught in introductory business classes. My session went okay, people played along, engaged and humored me, but then the evaluations came.

On a Likert scale I was ranked average, sometimes below, and the comments reaffirmed the belief that my tangible takeaway was simply too basic for the audience. Some even went as far as to insult me as a practitioner, stating that I must not have a clue about strategy or business.

The Who

To be truthful, for me, strategy came second and I could even argue that it came naturally. Because what I know and what I've always known is people. And it is when you know who makes up an organization, that you have the power to manifest change within them. I believe that failing to recognize "the who" has led us to where we are today.

Whether it is massive diversity initiatives, high turnover rates, toxic work environments and a new generation with a set of demands and a new level of entitlement. We did this! We created the current chaos because we forgot "the who."

So it doesn't matter that you have read the latest and greatest business books or have been through hours and hours of continuing education on leadership development and philosophy. If you are not being taught how the tools or theory can be used to learn about "the who," you are missing the biggest factor when it comes to strategy, period.

There I was, frustrated, angry, and hurt by the comments. How do I share exactly what I do as a very respected and successful practitioner to only be laughed at? That's when I realized what had happened. I hadn't been completely honest with myself or those people. There is something else at work when I utilize a simple tool like a SWOT analysis. Something else that I never talked about because I was afraid of being laughed at.

But I was already being laughed at, so what did I have to lose? For years when I would do my work with people, I noticed that I had a bit of an uncanny ability to connect with and know people. Being an HR practitioner, that ability proved particularly helpful. But it is this skill set that makes the simple tools like a SWOT analysis powerful and almost magical. Therefore, before we go any further, there is something that I need to put out there and own:

I'm a highly intuitive empath.

What does that mean? To put it extremely simply, I have intense gut feelings combined with an intense ability to understand other people's emotions. Therefore, when I say things like, "I have a bad feeling about this," or "I totally get what you're feeling," I do.

It took a long time for me to accept that these abilities existed for me, and for most of my life I assumed they were abilities that everyone had. But as I wrote my first book, *From Heart to HRart*, the puzzle pieces of my life, and more importantly who I am, started to fall into place. This triggered many emotions including a lot of shame and a lot of fear. I also had a sort of awakening, knowing that this journey of self-discovery had provided me with findings that I could never unfind.

Can You Read?

In my family, there is an old story that morphed into a playful inside joke with my father. My memories are filled with the amount of joy this particular incident brought my father every time we referenced it.

The event happened at a dentist's office during one of my early childhood routine cleanings. For the entire year my father had been displeased at my lack of flossing. He was even more irritated by my continued excellent record at the dentist because this shouldn't be possible since I didn't floss. Not flossing should almost be an instant disqualifier from having a "good visit" at the dentist.

After the dentist gave me accolades once again for my perfect pearly whites, she went on to deliver the good news to my father while I got my fluoride treatment. Later, I would learn that my father shared with the dentist that he wouldn't hear about my impeccable pearly whites because I didn't floss. The dentist was shocked to learn this and assured my father that she would speak with me about the significance of flossing.

When the dental hygienist returned for what was supposed to be me picking out the bubble gum flavored fluoride, she instead came in and said that they were just informed that I do not floss regularly. I owned up to it and admitted that I rarely if ever did. This was then proceeded with a personal demonstration of how to floss on a gigantic plastic imitation mouth. It was followed by the hygienist presenting me with a pamphlet on flossing and inquiring in a loud very emphasized drawn out manner by asking, "*CAN YOU READ?*" I confusingly responded yes and took the pamphlet.

I later shared this story with my family and my father found it hilarious. For years we would shout back and forth to each other, "*CAN YOU READ?*" And although I never truly knew the reason behind her chosen vocal tone and question, this story reminds me of my own awakening—a disconnect that was present, that I assumed was present for everyone else as well.

Our culture has rules, standards, and best practices for life. One may even argue that flossing is one of these best practices. Joking aside, flossing is important, and believe me when I say that dental karma bit me in the ass in adulthood. But forget that for the moment. For the sake of my point, in this story I went against a cultural norm and flourished. It came natural to me and yet the instinctual reaction was to attempt to break me and mold me to external expectations. If I had wanted to process this story through a dark place, I could say they humiliated me with their ridiculous childlike display and offensive assumption of my lack of reading comprehension. In addition, we could probably overanalyze my father's actions, wondering why he couldn't simply be happy to have a healthy little girl. Why was it necessary to nitpick and push further?

I use this example because I know I am not the only one who rebels in regard to this best life practice of flossing. I know many of my close friends and family who, to this day, still have never had any sort of practice flossing. (No worries, no call outs in this book.) These individuals have gone against the expectation and still flourished in their own way. They have done so while holding onto this secret, that they don't floss.

I want you to realize that my highly intuitive and empathic gifts are about as special as flossing. It is a talent that I have, a gift that has empowered me to live my why. But it is also a gift or ability that everyone has if they choose to develop it. Being a highly sensitive introverted child just equipped me with a natural tendency to let these abilities flourish.

Embracing Intuition

Recently I had the opportunity to interview my first holistic life coach, Kara Lovehart, on the podcast regarding the topic of being an Empath. Kara was the obvious choice since she had helped me greatly in navigating the discovery of my own empathic abilities.

When I first began working with Kara, I had convinced myself that I was experiencing an awakening of abilities, after I had successfully made them dormant as a child. During our interview, Kara shared something that she had never said to me directly during our coaching sessions. "Our intuitive skill sets can never truly be suppressed indefinitely." They will continue to find a way to the surface. It is when we choose to take on the impossible task of attempting to make them disappear, that we begin the journey of denying all that we truly are. To do this takes a great amount of energy that can never be sustained, and therefore, after time, we begin to lose hold and it finds a way to make its presence known.

This process sounds like a beautiful release, however if you do the math right, the equation of when we begin to lose the strength of constantly hiding who we are, hits its tipping point in early adulthood, just as we are beginning our professional lives. Could this possibly explain the difference between clear childhood dreams of what we want to be when we grow up and the horrible lost sense of direction many of us experience upon entering the workforce?

It is this inevitable leak of intuitive skill sets that has ignited the core of my work, fixing the deep-ripple denial in our organizations and our lives. However, simply accepting the existence of these skills sets is not the end of the story. These skill sets, like any other, need parameters to flourish. Without parameters, intuition becomes more like an invasive chaotic weed in the garden. However, establishing intention allows for cultivation to sprout beautiful blossoms or magnificent branches.

I always believed accepting the intuitive gifts would be my greatest challenge, but when my coaching relationship ended with Kara, she left me to ponder what I wanted to use these skills for. It was a question that I had no idea how to answer. The traditional responses, of conducting readings and life coaching, seemed irrelevant to my professional aspirations. My initial reaction was narrow-minded and the question Kara posed was the initial seed that I've been cultivating for five years. This book outlines the mighty root system to a tree of wisdom that has laid dormant for too long.

The Dao

"The Chinese word *Dao* means a way or a path. Confucians used the term Dao to speak of the way human beings ought to behave in society."[1] When we think of individuals pursuing the Dao, it is natural to have visions of monks isolated in the mountains that meditate in silence for days. In fact, when I first began studying the art of Qigong, I believed that would be my fate inevitably as well. However, the true definition of the work brings to light that the Dao is merely an intentional path, a methodology, you might say, for how we should function in life. For me, my work is about bringing the Dao to Human Resources.

The way in which HR works with people, and its lack of Dao, has caused the current state of crisis we are seeing universally in workspaces, one that is causing employees to revolt, believing that they must become their own personal advocate because the organization is too disconnected from humanity. That is why I believe it is time for an HR revolution, one where those of us who have been called to this work step up and embrace what we were always meant to be.

Historically, HR evolved out of a need to complete tasks that were overwhelming to organizational management. The commonality of these tasks was that they all revolved around people. The birth of the HR profession was the first recognition that people were a significant source of energy for companies. People provided essential energy to the organization but also required energy as well.

A great balance between give and take was necessary to create an environment where both parties benefited. That lack of balance is what has now resulted in a broken base compensation system, non-inclusive work environments that hinder authenticity, as well as

---

[1]http://afe.easia.columbia.edu/special/china_1000bce_daoism.htm

legislation that requires black-and-white policies. HR was intended to be the great caretaker of organizational energy. This essential aspect of the role was never realized because the significance of its impact was always severely underestimated. Now in a world where no one wants to work, many accept that things cannot continue as before, yet are lost as to where to start.

This is a powerful unique window of opportunity that has presented itself to HR, yet practitioners are too tired and overwhelmed to even consider the option to seize this moment. In fact, many have even given in to the internal calls to retreat and restore personally, exiting the profession all together... while those barely holding it together feel helpless in providing a genuine hope that it will one day get better or at least lighter.

Healing is Necessary

Before we can begin thinking about the Dao in HR, healing is in order. The toll that the current environment has taken by people must be undone in an act that will restore us to a time when we had the energy to work. Life is one large energy exchange, with little to no training on how to care for our personal energy. We hear loose references to it, by being encouraged to establish boundaries, or make time for self-care, even the emphasis placed on the importance of physical rest. However, there is no true training on how to care for your energetic outputs and inputs.

If you notice, I referenced that this healing and restoration is necessary for us. We as practitioners are included—in fact, it has to start there because we are the only ones who can facilitate the organizational healing needed around the world. But we cannot facilitate until we have healed and restored ourselves. This is what this book is for—guiding you to heal and restore yourself while then giving you a taste of what it will be like to be a powerful catalyst in the healing of others. My hope is the taste of healing power will inspire you to continue your own personal cultivation and open your eyes to what the working world could be like once the Dao is present.

While I often speak to HR practitioners specifically, know that I view the definition much more broadly. In fact, my belief is that all of leadership is part of HR and therefore leading people will require a healing skill set as well.

Our Tree of Wisdom

In 2011, the city of Rikuzentakata, Japan, was completely devastated by a tsunami. All that was left was one pine tree. This tree became a symbol of resilience and re-awakening. If you are still reading this, you are resilient and are re-awakening. You are still standing because you know there is more and this is the missing wisdom you have been seeking.

This book will share this wisdom in three levels. Three spiritual animal guides will help us to provide insight on the scope and intention of these levels, which are stacked in vertical fashion. Our animal friends are sitting in a pine tree and your growth throughout this book will climb this tree, greeting each one respectively as you evolve.

The Groundhog

We begin on the ground with the groundhog. The groundhog invites us to find answers within, by burrowing deeply. It is often said that when you dream of a groundhog, it represents subconscious information coming to the surface. Therefore, this level is all about uncovering what you already know but have yet to verbalize or acknowledge.

A huge component of this level is awakening your intuitive skill set—what my book *The HR Intuitive* is all about. For our purposes here, we will burrow deep into the current state of organizational HR personalities and how they manifest. Understanding why we function the way we do on a daily basis creates a primer for further exploration and evolution.

The Mourning Dove

Hidden halfway up somewhere in the branches, the mourning dove awaits. The mourning dove represents peace and power. It provides a sign of hope to those that have been suffering. It represents the value your healing capacity will bring to your employees. In part two, we will begin the act of cleansing and cultivation that will enable you to utilize your healing power. In addition, this process will allow you to experience a personal sense of peace and hope that you've been craving.

The Hawk

Up in the tippy top of the tree sits the hawk, watching and waiting. Many say that hawks represent a spiritual awareness, accompanied with the gift of sight. When hawks serve as a spirit animal for individuals, they are known for intelligence, adaptability, and independence. The hawk, for us, represents what is possible when the Dao is present in HR. This is something that I have yet to fully see myself, as we are deep in the trenches of healing work before we are able to truly vision.

The hawk represents what's to come, what we will be and the way we will do it.

PART ONE

THE GROUNDHOG
SHARES OUR CAUSE

CHAPTER ONE

WHAT'S YOUR HR PERSONALITY?

The first question that reasonably comes to your mind is likely, "Do we all have an HR personality?" I would argue there are three qualifiers that nearly guarantee you have an HR personality. Which of the following statements rings true for you?

1. You actively work in an HR Profession, have worked in an HR Profession or intend/hope to work in an HR Profession.

2. You actively work in a formal managerial or leadership profession or have had previous experience in a role where you had to supervise a team of people.

3. Yours is an organization that cannot survive without people, in other words you cannot function strictly off of AI bots.

Yes, there are three ways that an HR Personality manifests—two at the individual level, and a third within an organization. Leaders and HR Professionals each possess or develop an HR Personality and so do organizations. This personality essentially dictates our common approach to how we manage people.

What is HR?

> *"Human Resource Management is the term generally applied to those activities concerning the management of people."*

This definition of HR was found in a textbook, one I highly recommend, if you are looking to obtain a solid foundation—*Human Resource Management* by Robert L. Mathis and John H. Jackson. At first, I was critical of this definition, but then I realized the necessity for vagueness. Despite, the length of time Human Resources has been around as an industry and profession, we are still figuring out who exactly we are within the organizations we serve.

Sure, we take care of administrative tasks surrounding people who work for an organization (i.e., hiring, firing). But that is not all we do. We are involved with every activity concerning people within our organizations, and in situations where we are not involved, we should be asking why not. It is in these situations where "we" (as in HR) are not involved that another person must inevitably become the voice of a missing strategic partner. This other voice is often one of a leader, or manager. It is the simple yet frequent act of leaving the organic organizational need for HR vacant for too long that ultimately creates an HR Personality within these leaders.

What is a Personality?

The American Psychological Association defines personality as:

> *"Personality refers to individual differences in characteristic patterns of thinking, feeling, and behaving. The study of personality focuses on two broad areas: One is understanding individual differences in particular personality characteristics, such as sociability or irritability. The other is understanding how the various parts of a person come together as a whole."* [2]

The moment an organization decides to hire its first employee, an HR personality is born. Organizations are created with missions and visions dancing in the entrepreneur's head—hopes and dreams of what will be accomplished and how it will one day change the world.

---

[2] https://www.apa.org/topics/personality

Part of these hopes and dreams comes with the recognition that to make them come true, the entrepreneur will not be able to do it alone. One day they will need a team.

As entrepreneurs and leaders, we must also develop missions and visions for our teams, how we want them to function, and how we want them to grow. It is these missions and visions aligned with the ones that established the organization that begin to dictate the patterns of how we think, feel, and behave when it comes to managing our people. These same patterns express yet another level of individuality that makes our culture uniquely ours and generates the necessary dynamics of how we truly come together to accomplish our goals.

Okay, What is Mine?

Before we continue, it is important to understand your or your organizational HR Personality. To determine this, you will complete a short assessment which includes seven questions, asking what you would do in certain scenarios. The questions are framed from an HR practitioner perspective; however, this should not deter you if you do not actively serve in an HR profession.

To discover your HR Personality, you simply need to answer the seven questions as you would navigate them in your current leadership role. If your goal is to determine the organization's HR Personality, answer the questions from the perspective of how your ideal HR practitioner would navigate these scenarios in your organization.

If you are someone who aspires to one day work in HR, simply approach the assessment from the perspective of what you believe your response would be in that given situation.

As with any assessment, the results will be best if you do not overthink your responses. Go with your initial thoughts because this assessment is largely based on intuitive factors.

The Assessment

On the pages that follow, answer the seven questions by ranking your responses, with a score of either 1, 2, or 3.

- A score of **1** means this would be your **most likely response** to the given situation.

- A score of **2** means this would be your **second most likely response** to the given situation.

- A score of **3** means this would be your **least likely response** to the given situation.

1. When you first start your workday, *what is the first thing you have a tendency to do?*

    a. I typically start making rounds throughout the workplace with the intention to build and maintain meaningful relationships. __

    b. I typically start making rounds throughout the workplace with the intention to check in with everyone. __

    c. I typically start working on tasks that need to be completed immediately. __

2. An irate employee storms into your office screaming that their benefits are wrong. They received a bill from the doctor that they believe should have been covered and assume it is an error you must have made. When the employee is finished with their tirade, *what do you do?*

   a. I resist the urge to avoid the situation and instead focus on finding a creative solution to address their concern while restoring trust with the employee. __

   b. I thoroughly explore if the conflict has to be addressed by me or identify if another party is best to respond. __

   c. I reactively confront the employee with facts and address their issue directly to eliminate the problem. __

3. You just attended a fantastic conference that inspired and motivated you. You return to work filled with great ideas on how to update old policies and enact changes to make the organization stronger. You prepare a proposal to Leadership and it gets rejected. *What do you do?*

   a. I utilize the strong relationships I have already built within the organization to help me position the proposal with support, so it is implemented. __

   b. I believe that if the proposal was denied that they had a valid reason not to implement it and I let the issue go. __

   c. I continue to be persistent in explaining why change is needed in hopes of swaying their opinion. This could include additional research and fact-finding to strengthen my case. __

4. You are in the middle of working on a big special project, but need to leave by 5:00 P.M. to attend your personal evening plans. You realize you will not be able to finish the project if you leave at that time. The project isn't technically due today, but it would be largely beneficial to have it completed before the deadline. *What do you do?*

   a. I see if I can rearrange my personal plans so I can stay and finish. ___

   b. It isn't due today, so I will leave at 5:00. ___

   c. I determine with my current workload and schedule if I can have time to complete it by the deadline. If I can, I leave at 5:00, but if not, I stay late to complete it. ___

5. Your organization has always had the practice that managers write and document performance issues for their own employees. HR is supposed to review all documentation and formal counselings prior to them being issued. Your supervisor recently informed you that moving forward, the organization has decided that HR should handle the entire process for addressing performance issues. The managers have a lot on their plate, and it was determined this was a task that could easily be delegated. *How do you respond?*

   a. I attempt to understand the new direction by identifying the connection of the change to the bigger picture and organizational vision. __

   b. I accept the additional responsibilities but am uncomfortable with the change. However, I do not express my dissatisfaction with the new organizational decision. __

   c. I need a clear understanding of the why behind this decision. If after knowing the why I determine this is a direction I can support, I embrace the change and move forward. __

6. An employee comes and tells you they are being harassed by their supervisor. They say they don't want the person to be fired, they just want it to stop. *What is your initial reaction?*

   a. I have high anxiety due to the empathy I feel for the employee having the issue. ___

   b. I feel stressed because of the nature of the situation and extra work that will be needed on top of my normal workload. ___

   c. I am ready to ask clarifying questions so I can address it accordingly and then move on. ___

7. Your company hired a temporary employee to serve as a Project Manager to evaluate the current HRIS system. This hired employee delivered on expectations. They did exactly what was asked of them and nothing more. Their supervisor reaches out to you and requests that you plan a nice thank you luncheon for this person. *How do you feel about this request?*

   a. I love any opportunity to recognize employees and I take the initial idea of a thank you lunch and find a way to make it especially special or better. __

   b. I like the idea but try to find a way to make it a general recognition lunch for all employees. __

   c. I have a hard time understanding why we would have a luncheon when all they did was the job we hired them to do. __

Scoring

Take a moment and translate your response rankings on the scorecard below.

For example, if I answered question number one as:

1. When you first start your workday, *what is the first thing you have a tendency to do?*

      a. I typically start making rounds throughout the workplace with the intention to build and maintain meaningful relationships. **2**

      b. I typically start making rounds throughout the workplace with the intention to check in with everyone. **1**

      c. I typically start working on the tasks that need to be completed immediately. **3**

I would record my responses on the score card as:

	Response A	Response B	Response C
Question 1	2	1	3

Once you have translated your response rankings onto the scorecard, add up your totals for each column. The column with the **lowest total** is your current dominant HR personality.

The Scorecard

	Response A	Response B	Response C
Question 1			
Question 2			
Question 3			
Question 4			
Question 5			
Question 6			
Question 7			
Totals			

Chapter Two

What Does It Mean?

I know the excitement was building as you turned the page to discover what exactly your score means, so here are the results. Remember it is based on your *lowest* score. The lettered column where you received the lowest score identifies your dominant HR Personality.

Drumroll please...

> If you received your *lowest* score in **column A**, you are a **Unicorn**.

> If you received your *lowest* score in **column B,** you are a **Phoenix**.

> If you received your *lowest* score in **column C**, you are a **Dragon**.

Now, what if your lowest score is the same in two columns? We will process the meaning of this in the next chapter but for now you can make note of yourself as a hybrid.

For example, if your lowest score tied in columns A and C, you are a *Unicorn* or *Dragon*, whichever you prefer.

Now that you know your HR Personality is tied to a mythical creature you potentially have three questions...

1. Why mythical creatures? And how in the world are they relevant to our profession?

2. How could I possibly be described as the mythical creature you identified me as, after this random personality assessment?

3. Does this assessment have any true purpose and validity?

I believe the answers to these questions will drastically assist in painting a picture as to why a healing practice is an essential and unavoidable evolution to our profession. In fact, I could argue it is long overdue, and the vacancy of this practice has been the true root cause to our organizational culture struggles.

If you are eager to learn more about your specific HR personality, have patience. That will all be addressed as I answer these questions. So, where to begin? I guess at the beginning—how did this whole concept even originate?

HR Besties

Gallup, a global analytics and advice firm that helps leaders and organizations solve their most pressing problems, has a common practice of asking a question regarding best friends at work during employee engagement research for organizations. This question has become one of the most controversial over the last 30 years of the organization's existence, yet it continues to be included. When asked why by clients, their answer is simple—*performance*. Their research "has repeatedly shown a concrete link between having a best friend at work and the amount of effort employees expend in their job. For example, women who strongly agree they have a best friend at work are more than twice as likely to be engaged (63%) compared with the women who say otherwise (29%)."[3]

According to Gallup, I am one of the two out of every 10 workers[4] who works with my BFF today. In fact, we found each other at work. There is an old saying that you don't pick HR as a career, HR

---

[3] https://www.gallup.com/workplace/236213/why-need-best-friends-work.aspx

[4] https://getlighthouse.com/blog/best-friend-at-work-bff/

chooses you, and I played a pretty significant role in delivering that message by choosing MaryRose.

At the time, I had just graduated from college after five super long years to obtain my bachelor's degree. I was working for a big box retailer and was offered a promotion into an HR Manager position. My only hurdle was that I needed to find my replacement. At the time I was working as the HR Coordinator, which predominantly acted as assistant to the store's HR Manager.

As I combed through applications of individuals seeking seasonal employment, one caught my eye. MaryRose was currently in law school seeking only a small amount of hours to supplement her schoolwork. The amount of hours she needed perfectly mirrored mine and the fact that she was pursuing law meant that she had to have at least a general understanding of confidentiality in the workplace. I leaped at the opportunity that she might be my answer, pushing my HR Manager and Store Manager to consider her. MaryRose ended up filling my position and I moved on to my own store.

A year went by and I was offered an opportunity to transition to a mid-size retailer as an HR Specialist that supported several stores from a corporate office environment. It wasn't long before that retailer started seeking additional HR support to keep up with company growth. And as fate would have it, MaryRose was the candidate who came recommended when I reached out to mutual HR colleagues. It was during our shared time at this retailer when we truly established a close relationship.

This friendship with MaryRose works because of the balance we bring each other. This balance creates the perfect arena to vet ideas and opinions on complete randomness. It was in this arena of randomness that the concept of the HR Personality was born.

When it comes to how we approach our work, the thought process is pretty much the same for me and MaryRose, but the skillsets where we thrive are polar opposites. Despite that we both are capable of managing all aspects of HR, just like our colleagues we each have areas where we particularly excel. For MaryRose, these areas are centered on risk management and compliance. For me, it's creativity and culture.

Our HR Personalities are rooted in the areas of HR that we tend to focus on, regardless of whether that focus is due to work demand or personal preference.

As we began discussing the concept of HR Personalities, MaryRose became the prototype for the Dragon personality and I became the prototype for the Unicorn Personality. With these two personalities vaguely identified, we recognized that a third personality was inevitable. We knew there was an approach a few of our colleagues shared that was unlike ours, and these individuals became the prototype for the third and final personality, Phoenix.

Creating An Assessment, then Testing Its Validity and Reliability

Despite my desire and intention to continue expanding our scope and research into these personalities and what they mean, I believe it is important to share that this assessment is still actively evolving. However, even in its infancy, it has provided valuable insight that has already established a case for the healing practice of HR.

The assessment you experienced is comprised of seven situational questions. These scenarios reflect times when the vast differences of personalities could be observed, within myself, MaryRose and the collective of colleagues who serve as the prototype for the Phoenix. In fact, the responses accurately depict the way each of us has reacted in the past.

To test our initial HR Personality theory, we invited 10 of our close HR colleagues to complete the assessment and share their results. This group included colleagues we have known for several years as well as the individuals who served as the Phoenix prototype.

Prior to receiving their results, MaryRose and I hypothesized who we believed would be classified as each personality. When the results returned we had accurately predicted all 10. We then shared with the group the descriptions associated with their dominant personality result and asked if they believed the description was accurate. The resounding feedback was *yes*, even when it was a reluctant yes.

After a successful small pilot, we were eager to share and receive more feedback. As of 2020, we have had 250 professionals complete the HR Personality assessment and the results have been overwhelmingly accurate, with only a handful of outliers who have disagreed with their results. Once again, by no means is this scientific, however it is enough to establish that there are patterns of behavior in our work approach as HR professionals.

Personality Characteristics

The table below lists characteristics that describe each of the HR Personalities…

Dragon	Unicorn	Phoenix
Impatient	Highly independent	Beautiful radiance
Eccentric	Elusive	Warm nature
Helpers	Able to blend in	Solitary
Rarely asks for help	Innocent	Aloof
Colorful personality	Noble	Reserved
Prefers to be alone	Pure-hearted	Virtuous
Unafraid of challenges	Likes companions	Respects supervisors
Willing to take risks	Powerful	Helpful to others
Ambitious	Healing	A brilliant death of its own making
Agile	Nurturer	Rebirth
Cunning	Mysterious	Able to recover from setbacks
Driven	Intuitive	Compassionate
Likes own rules	Vibrant imagination	Hopeful
Not discouraged by difficulties	Sense of wonder	
Hates being used/controlled		
Passionate		
Passion can make them exhausted		
Does things in a grand fashion		
Tempers can flare fast		
Leaders		
Try for perfection		
Energetic		
Excitable		
Tactless		
Magnanimous		
Hates hypocrisy		
Dominate		

HR as Mythical Creatures

Dictionary.com defines the word *mythical* as:

*an adjective pertaining to,
of the nature of, or involving a myth*

It is also defined as:

without foundation in fact;
imaginary; fictitious.

Myth, by definition, is any invented story, idea, or concept. It is an imaginary or fictitious thing or person.

In business, still today, Human Resources and the possibility of what our partnership can bring to an organization is considered by many to be a myth. In fact, I believe our heavy focus on compliance is partially due to an attempt at establishing a foundation in facts. But when we get to concepts of doing what is right for employees or the argument of why culture is critical to success, we are often challenged to prove our insights. This has resulted in HR Dashboards populated with numbers and formulas all created by HR Practitioners attempting to link what we do to organizational data— a necessary practice if we truly want to navigate political dynamics within our organizations and manifest change.

What we do and how we see the business landscape is a skillset that is neither imaginary nor fictitious, but essential. We work with the unseen and often unsaid, because our skillset is embedded in understanding the human element of our businesses. We are challenged to understand that human element and know how to utilize it to magnify the organization's desired outcomes. We are so much more than hiring and firing. We are so much more than party coordinators. We are mystical beings who can foster an organization's resiliency driven by the people. But to do so, we require trust and belief from our leaders, not skepticism and resistance. Until HR is universally welcomed as a trusted partner, and believed in to make significant contributions, we will remain a myth to all but a few. Those few are the leaders who know that HR is not an isolated required position, that they too are HR and equally responsible for those within their organization. They also have seen glimpses of what could be if we embrace the human element.

The Dragon

The Dragon is without a doubt the most common HR Personality. Even if the Unicorn or Phoenix was your dominant personality result, it is probably likely that the Dragon is a close second. This quote by Elena Harris, the Editor of SpiritAnimal.info, describes perfectly why this is:

> *"The Dragon is cloaked with mystique and sewn together by the many legends and folklore surrounding its history. This powerful and mesmerizing creature has been the inspiration for many. The Dragon has been well respected in many cultures and is either honored or greatly feared."*

I was raised in my HR career by Dragons, as many of us were. Our HR mentors and role models were Dragons. These were the professionals who gained respect and established a sometimes necessary intimidation factor to get things done. In fact, we have begun to see a few trends specific to the Dragon personality in our assessment participants. The first is directly tied to the maturity level within the position, so there is a clear difference between the Dragon with 10 years of experience versus the Baby Dragon who has perhaps only three years. In addition, there is something to be said for the driving factor that created the Dragon personality—some Dragons are made, while others are that way because of their innate nature.

As you can see in the Personality Characteristics chart, the Dragon possesses a large number of traits. Elena Harris continues: "Dragon has a diverse range of qualities, emotions, and traits, giving it a number of different meanings. Most often it carries a reminder of strength, courage, and fortitude. Dragons are messengers of balance and magic. It is the master of all elements: fire, water, air, and earth. As a spirit guide, it makes a powerful ally in our daily life with its amazing restorative and potent qualities."[5]

---

[5] https://www.spiritanimal.info/dragon-spirit-animal/

Dragons are the embodiment of the HR Generalist position, and they commonly are the HR Department of one. In 2015, Society for Human Resource Management (SHRM) released a report sharing that almost 10% of their 275,000 members work in companies with fewer than 100 people, and many are the only HR presence. Dragons often out of necessity serve as daily guides, putting out fires and attempting to maintain a balance of limiting risk in a constantly evolving environment, both internally and externally. Since this is the common landscape for the Dragon, I'd like to take a moment to highlight a few specific behaviors and their potential causes.

Impatient/Tempers Can Flare Fast

Dragons have a tendency to quickly become irritated or provoked. This behavior is driven by the consistent demand placed on them to prove themselves. Dragons often function in a work environment where the value of HR must be established. Most are pioneering this charge, therefore, their daily interactions consist of constant questioning, even on subjects where a Dragon has demonstrated their effectiveness. This leads to obvious frustration, creating a communication technique experienced as short, cold, and irate.

Unafraid Of Challenges and Willing To Take Risks

Dragons understand the potential payoff for tackling challenges head-on and strategically embracing risk. Commonly these challenges are presented from individuals who have a lack of understanding when it comes to HR strategy, and therefore the risk presented in these situations is more so one of a potentially conflict-infused outcome. Conflict often arises out of disagreement about how a particular situation should be managed and whether the recommended action by the Dragon is truly serving the principles and interest expressed by the managing party.

Passionate, But Passion Can Make Them Exhausted

Dragons routinely charge into challenges and tolerate the incessant questioning of their recommendations because of their passion for people. Underneath the behaviors that have had to surface as a result of the environment, is an individual who indisputably believes in the value of people. This passion serves as a fire that must burn unceasingly. It is simply unreasonable to not expect these individuals to succumb to the inevitable burnout. It is at these times that we often encounter a Dragon with a general numbness to their environment, running on low energetic reserves but attempting to not halt their progress.

Likes Own Rules

As previously mentioned, Dragons often function in work environments where prior to their existence, little to no credible HR practices were established. Therefore, they default to creating their own processes and procedures or "rules." These processes and procedures are typically a cumulation of tried and true practices they have witnessed while being mentored by a fellow Dragon.

Magnanimous and Hates Hypocrisy

After reviewing the previous three behaviors and their causes, it is probably no surprise that Dragons are generous or forgiving of their adversaries in the workplace. This trait is almost a necessity if a Dragon is ever truly going to be capable of manifesting organizational change. With that being said, a Dragon is rarely magnanimous toward an individual whose claimed integrity is in question. A Dragon can understand an individual attempting to function from a genuine place of integrity, however those who have been exposed as strictly speaking a good game will fall from grace and find it challenging to redeem themselves in the Dragon's eye.

The Unicorn

> *"The unicorn is the most ambiguous and poetic*
> *of all beasts of fable."*
> —*Garth C. Clifford*

For our purposes, we will explore the Unicorn personality by the believed symbolism of this mythical creature in Chinese legend and Celtic beliefs.

The Chinese unicorn is called a *Qilin*—pronounced *chee-leen*. In Buddhist depictions of the Qilin, the creature is often shown walking on clouds, reiterating its gentle and peaceful nature by not even wanting to harm a single blade of grass by walking on it. Other stories share that the Qilin can incinerate people, but these stories also reiterate that the creature only does so to "defend innocent people from the malice of evil-doers." It is also believed that the Qilin would only appear during the reign of a good ruler, or shortly before the birth or death of a sage.[6]

The Unicorn HR Personality is the second most dominant. However, the number of dominant Unicorn personality results is significantly less than the number of dominant Dragon results. Typically 60% of HR Practitioners receive a dominant Dragon personality result, where Unicorns make up only about 35%. This statistic is not surprising, given the fact that Unicorns can only appear when organizational leadership allows. In fact, the number is potentially higher now than ever, due to the growing trend concerning employee engagement.

Just like the true mythical creature, in the world of business it is debated if the Unicorn's work is substantial, realistic, or even necessary. Therefore, a trend is emerging where Unicorns appear under great leaders, or right before an organization evolves toward greatness. We also have seen Unicorns present in work environments where their existence is unquestioned and viewed as essential. The Unicorn HR personality is fully aligned and embedded in the organizational culture.

When observing the Unicorn's approach to work it could be described as gentle in nature, especially when directly compared to the Dragon's approach. But do not underestimate the power and

---

[6] https://www.ancient-origins.net/myths-legends-asia/gentle-and-benevolent-qilin-chinese-mythology-001933

effectiveness of what is occurring in these light, gradual, and even easy actions. A Unicorn enters a work landscape with the intention of creating an environment for people to flourish. Unicorns focus their energy predominantly on culture development for an organization as well as exposing individuals who attempt to counteract the organization's values and vision.

From a Celtic perspective, I want to share with you one specific belief. Celtics "believed that the unicorn could take one look at another person and know his heart and whether they were virtuous."[7] This is a skillset that Unicorns are indeed capable of, because the majority of how a Unicorn works is by utilizing intuition. Unicorns have active intuitive senses, each with varying degrees of strength depending on the individual. Yet, as a Unicorn is able to be truly embraced rather than challenged, these intuitive senses only become stronger.

Now let's take a moment and explore a few of the common Unicorn HR Personality traits.

Able To Blend In

The Unicorn thrives when their work is focused on culture cultivation. It is utilizing their ability to blend in that allows them to establish the powerful foundation for the work. A Unicorn is able to navigate organizational political dynamics with ease. The Unicorn enters an organization with a sole initial intent to know the current state and appreciate the active depths of development. The Unicorn is only able to obtain their desired level of understanding by entering a practice of observation that requires a seamless travel throughout the current organizational structure as they deem necessary.

Healing

The Unicorn recognizes the complexity that encompasses an individual. They know on some level that each person is doing the

---

[7] https://www.worldbirds.org/unicorn-symbolism

best they can given their circumstances at the time. In order to generate the growth desired by organizations, the Unicorn has concluded that employee wellness must be a considered factor. In addition, the Unicorn has felt a pull to continue expanding on the definition of wellness in the workplace. There is a sense of knowing that the practice of healing and restoration is inevitable when it comes to any work involving people.

Nurturer

This trait often manifests as people-pleasing but is rooted in a strong response to a need—the need from individuals in the workspace to feel a genuine sense of care. They hold a belief that the organization is committed to fostering the individuals they hire because of an authentic appreciation for who they are as people and the work that they do. The overall common lack of this caring characteristic within cultures causes the Unicorn to naturally gravitate toward an approach of looking after others fairly quickly.

Intuitive

An intuitive operates in the realm of things often not seen or recognized, due to a lack of sensitivity to the surroundings. This skillset is not magical and is one that everyone possesses. Unfortunately it is often underdeveloped or subconsciously blocked. The Unicorn utilizes these skills to craft organizational strategies centered on people. Their intuitive nature often materializes as an intuitive sense, the act of seeing, hearing, feeling, or knowing things without the presence of evidence on which we have become heavily accustomed to relying.

Vibrant Imagination

Unicorns are known for their creativity, which is frequently accompanied with high optimism. Their ideas and visions will often take a minute to understand, but do not discourage them from sharing. This sadly is the trait that mostly remains hidden, because Unicorns have learned that our workspaces are not yet ready for the concepts that dance through their heads. If anything, a Unicorn typically gives glimpses of their creative nature but you have to wonder what could be possible if this creature was able to be fully transparent.

The Phoenix

In Chinese mythology, the Phoenix is known as the Feng-Huang, a bird much like a peacock but with a fiery red tail. The Feng Huang represents yin and yang energy or balance.[8]

Many are familiar with the myth of the Phoenix, a beautiful bird that rises time and again from its ashes. It is commonly associated with themes of rebirth and persistence. But when it comes to the HR Personality, these amazing individuals represent hope while bringing much needed balance.

The Phoenix has many faces and their landscape varies a great deal. Phoenixes can function in practically any work environment, surviving for many years. Some work for leaders who believe HR is worthless, treating them as well as their employees as such. The Phoenix stays despite its comprehension that change is unlikely. It is the loyalty to those they serve on a daily basis that drives their organizational commitment.

Others are working in organizations amidst great tragedy or failure, trying their best to be a source of hope when it seems impossible. These individuals have been known to go down with the ship proudly, or have sacrificed themselves in hope of inspiring change. It is safe to say that being a Phoenix is not for the faint of heart, which is why they comprise less than 10% of all results. I hold a deep respect for these individuals and the work they do.

Now that you have an idea of the circumstances that often surround a Phoenix, let's look at a few of their personality characteristics a bit closer.

---

[8] https://www.worldbirds.org/phoenix-symbolism/

Aloof

After learning a few of the scenarios that Phoenixes often find themselves in, I think you can understand why they periodically must disconnect. To others they may appear cold and distant, however this is strictly a survival technique to sustain the Phoenix as they face continual challenges.

Reserved

It is likely that a Phoenix has experienced consequences from previous passionate rants and as a result they now are slow to reveal their true emotions and opinions. This behavior is strategic in nature, as their main priority is to protect themselves and their employees.

Respects Supervisors

The Phoenix acknowledges organizational structure and regardless of whether they agree or disagree with a leader's philosophy, they will remain respectful. The Phoenix in this circumstance emulates the respect they one day hope to see this leader exhibit, attempting to be the model.

A Brilliant Death of Its Own Making

When the Phoenix experiences an ending in employment, whether voluntary or not, every time it is ignited by the Phoenix itself. The Phoenix always has a distinct decision that initiates the timeline leading to its brilliant death. In addition, the ending always has a defined purpose that is driven by growth for the organization or the individual.

Rebirth

Each time the Phoenix rises from the ashes, it is stronger. The Phoenix evolves with each rebirth, however this is not often instantly clear to the Phoenix. Frequently, the initial stages of rebirth are a time of transition and exploration as the Phoenix determines next steps.

Your Personal HR Personality Blend

Unless you scored a zero in any of the personality types, you are not actually one personality but a combination of all three. Your blend is truly unique to you as an individual and consists of your innate nature as well as external factors from the work landscape.

It is now time for us to discuss why it matters. But before we begin, it is important to fully appreciate the blend of HR Personalities that make up you. To do so, I recommend the following:

1. Take a look at the personality traits for each type. Taking into consideration those traits associated with your dominant personality type(s) but also those associated with the other types where you scored points.

2. Identify which characteristics describing your HR Personality are ones you agree with.

3. Identify any characteristics you initially disagreed with, but hesitated because you know they could possibly be true.

4. Think about what personal stories came to mind as you read the personality descriptions.

5. If you had to define your HR Personality, what would it be? Write it out.

CHAPTER THREE

WHAT'S THE POINT?

After the initial excitement settles from the act of discovering your mythical creature, it is inevitable to ask, "So what?" Regardless of people's inability to argue that a pattern is present to dictate these personality classifications, the question remains, does it really serve any true relevance or significance?

My motives were never to create a classification system for HR professionals. My intention was to continue my research regarding the challenges faced while creating engagement within our organizations. My work has led me to realize that if we are ever to have the ability to successfully increase and sustain engaged workforces, it begins with HR.

A concept that is not completely foreign, we have seen the natural tendency for organizational leaders to delegate the hefty tasks surrounding cultural development to their HR function. Please do not get me wrong. The nature of those tasks should be driven and managed by HR. The conflict that arises is that for the most part the HR profession has been groomed by organizational leadership to focus its energies on limiting risk, overseeing compliance, and completing administrative personnel functions. The HR skillsets that are essential to meet the challenge of successfully navigating culture development to boost company loyalty have been suppressed and actually dormant for years, even decades for certain professionals.

It is only after a 20-year trend, of little to no change in employee engagement numbers, that we are now discovering that something is potentially missing from our business strategies. It is only after the staggering data was released from study after study, that by 2020 the workforce will heavily lean toward self-employment rather than working for an organization they cannot trust. We have now compounded this 2020 data with a pandemic that has generated unforeseen circumstances. We essentially have a perfect storm— employees gifted with time for reflection, living in a literal pause of life, becoming accustomed to a type of work life and environment that has never been the norm.

The Meaning of 20

It's hard to read that previous paragraph and not see all the 20s right in your face. The year 2020 was history making. If you research the meaning and symbolism behind the number 20, you have to first appreciate the individual numbers and what they share before they combine for a powerful message, echoed in 2020 with the literal reiteration of the number in pattern form.

The number "2" symbolizes balance, harmony, teamwork, relationships, and adaptability. For our purposes, this number represents dormant skills of HR practitioners that must awaken. The number "0" is known to symbolize Divine energy. For our reference, that energy—regardless of your belief system—is the guiding force fueled by our purpose. When these two numbers combine to create "20," they symbolize the beginning of a spiritual journey.[9]

When we hear the word *spiritual* it is normal to drift to thoughts relating to religion. However, I would like you to consider the broader definition that includes a sense of connection to something bigger than ourselves. The number "20" signifies that the time is now to awaken our intuitive skillsets that allow us to bring balance, harmony, and purpose to our organizations. It instills in us the ability to connect with people in a necessary, intimate way that fosters relationships to reestablish the trust we have been seriously lacking

---

[9] https://angelnumbersmeaning.com/angel-number-20-meaning-and-symbolism/

in our professional lives—the trust that allows us to show up authentically, confident that we will be embraced and accepted. Instead we are trained to show up in a specific way, conducting ourselves in a manner that is dictated as "common sense"... and if we fail to do so, we can expect to never experience a sense of genuine belonging in our workplace.

Ourselves Included

"Because true belonging only happens when we present our authentic, imperfect selves to the world, our sense of belonging can never be greater than our level of self-acceptance."
—*Dr. Brene Brown*

Dr. Brene Brown's work has begun paving the path for linking words like *vulnerability* and *shame* to leadership. Along with *intimacy*, *authenticity,* and *trust,* these words have been deemed inappropriate for the workplace for too long. In fact, it has been so long that we now automatically consider these words irrelevant to our professional development. In actuality, these words are exactly what we need right now if we have any hope of integrating them into the workforce. It begins with us.

We must learn to present ourselves authentically and completely. Those of us who are called to serve in Human Resources are drawn for a common reason—the people. Furthermore, those of us who excel in this profession, do so because we possess a particular set of skills. These skills allow us to see, hear, feel, and know people in ways often overlooked in the workplace.

It is this combination of skills and calling that birthed our profession but what we are capable of doing has always been accompanied with doubt. Our work is that of a few in a sea of operational-dominated minds and we were tasked to bring balance to these well-established hierarchies. It was inevitable that we would be told our place rather than embraced as the missing element that could shift the organization for the better.

This is the origin of our story as practitioners. Instead of defining, we were instructed—meaning our potential was immediately given limits. This is why those who feel called to serve in Human Resources are hindered from the start. The wholeness of what we have to offer is rarely embraced and an individual can only resist repression for so long before succumbing to coping strategies and eventually developing a numbness or coldness a commonly described characteristic of an experienced Dragon HR Personality.

My theory is that the large amount of Dragon HR Personality results is not indicative of who we are as professionals, but rather the path we have professionally been forced to travel. I believe a majority of Dragons are not innate, they are made. Organizations have created their own Dragons.

Are Dragons Born or Made?

As a fellow Unicorn, images of white puffy clouds, rainbows, and puppies dance in my head. However, I know that balance is an absolute necessity. For HR to have the capacity to achieve its fullest potential, a Unicorn is no more valuable than a Dragon. Yet if we want any true possibility at achieving our fullest potential we must be permitted to fully embrace and recognize our innate HR personality. Therefore, no longer can a Unicorn hide as a Dragon or Phoenix, like I did for years.

If your HR Personality score led you to identify as a Dragon, the following Personality Climate Check-In will allow you to discover whether your personality is innate or organizationally made.

Personality Climate Check-In

Answer the following four questions by selecting the first response that comes to mind.

1. Now that you have identified your current dominant HR Personality, do you believe your personality is a reflection of your innate nature or what you have become as a result of your career path?

a. It's my innate nature.

b. It's a direct result of my career path.

c. I'm not sure… maybe both.

2. Are the primary factors that influence your HR Personality more so internal (from within) or external (the environment)?

   a. Internal Factors

   b. External Factors

   c. Both

3. In your ideal working environment (aka dream HR job), do you believe you would still have this current dominant HR Personality?

   a. Absolutely!

   b. No way!

   c. I don't know

4. Is your current dominant HR Personality aligned with your organization in regard to strategic initiatives and overall operational priorities?

   a. Yes

   b. No

   c. Sometimes

If you scored mostly **As**, it is likely that the Dragon is your authentic HR personality.

If you scored mostly **B**s, it is likely that the Unicorn is your authentic HR personality.

If you scored mostly **C**s, it would be logical to think that you are a blend. However, the uncertainty theme throughout the C responses actually indicates that you are in a place of transition. Remember the Phoenix—this personality commonly represents a minority that encompasses many situations of rebirth and transformation. If you are indeed a Unicorn and you answered mostly Cs, my guess is that you are functioning in a work environment that actively represses your innate nature… and you are tired. You might even say you are losing hope and questioning why your effort or work even matters.

The truth is we have all been the Phoenix at one point or more in our career. Some of us spend years in this state while others maybe only experience it for minutes. These are the times when we question our work and its place in business.

What the Personalities Represent

These three personalities represent a model of the qualities an HR professional would possess to be successful in tackling specific organizational driven challenges. For example, the *Dragon* personality is a perfect match for an organization actively attempting to minimize risk, ensure compliance, and develop a system for accountability. *Unicorns* possess a mindset ideal for navigating culture change and cultivating organizational potential. The *Phoenix* has the patience and courage to break down barriers and inspire hope.

But to flourish in this model, we must heal ourselves. We must undo what has been done, the molding that has been sculpted by those who are not called to serve in HR. Those who do not fully comprehend the power that people possess within organizations cannot begin to grasp the skills necessary to channel this power.

I cannot help but wonder, looking at that exhausting list of Dragon traits, how many are truly rooted in their inherent nature? How many were the result of work requests and demands driven by what others expected?

We have been functioning for way too long based on expectations created by others who do not understand the work we do. As a result, we developed coping strategies and focused our energies on skills that received affirmation from our work environments. This included numbing tactics to quiet the whispers of our intuition.

This leads us to where our work must begin—exploring why you are here. Why in the world are you an HR professional?

Chapter Four

Why Are You Here?

I never intended to write a book. Sure, the idea of Samm the author sounded nice, but also unrealistic. I wasn't a big reader and I was only a writer when required for educational or professional purposes.

I knew it would be easy to default to my professional HR and Training background to write a book filled with tips and lessons encountered over the years. That might still be in my future, but it didn't feel right. First I wanted to share something vulnerable and heartfelt. I wanted to share something *foundational*.

From the beginning, I knew the stories I wanted to share. I recognized the experiences that had happened to me that needed to be in this book. They were some of the most challenging realizations I have had to date. These realizations were hard lessons about myself that were necessary for me to grow. They represented my foundation, a starting place to begin moving forward on a path that I could take with newfound confidence.

This first book was filled with heart from day one. In fact, it has transformed so much of my work. By providing the clarity I needed to understand that my work is heart work, I adapted this play on words by spelling heart as *HRart*. It's a combination of my HR background, my roots, and my company Leadership Arts

Associates. But it is so much more than a play on words. *HRart* to me is purpose, passion, people, possibility, and power.[10]

1. I am a Human Resources Practitioner who helps individuals believe they have a purpose—both within our organizations and in life.

2. I am a Human Resources Practitioner who helps individuals find their passion, and then I help them find ways to keep that fire burning brightly.

3. I am a Human Resources Practitioner who is devoted to people, recognizing that they are the number one asset of any organization. I also recognize they are people with a diversity that needs to be fostered.

4. I am a Human Resources Practitioner who believes in possibilities, in dreams, in visions, and in our ability to make them happen.

5. I am a Human Resources Practitioner who believes in power—an empowerment so strong and true that individuals bring their authentic voice to our organizations being aligned with our vision and values.

Connecting with our people is the future of the HR industry and if this mindset is not embraced by organizations then I feel called to equip individuals with the ability to be at their absolute best. That is what this book is all about: empowering you to work, live, and love all that you do.

> *"If we find ourselves with a desire that nothing in this world can satisfy, the most probable explanation is that we were made for another world."* —C.S. Lewis

---

[10] Excerpted below from *From Heart to HRart: Empowering You to Work, Live, and Love* (Year of the Book, 2018).

A Surprising Foundation

These foundational beliefs became the dramatic conclusion to *From Heart to HRart* that few ever read. Those who did, expressed confusion because the thing I didn't know when writing my first book was who I was writing for. My audience was nebulous and I was still heavily questioning my worthiness. Regardless of circumstances, the outcome was inevitable and I knew my five concluding statements served as a foundation but wasn't completely sure to what.

The process to expose this foundation included a level of vulnerability, sharing stories that had been truly instrumental in shaping who I am. Each story revealed an aspect of my answer to the question of "Why am I here? Why this path? Why this profession?"

When these five statements combine, they create the definition of what I have begun to call a *HRart worker*—a term used to describe predominantly HR practitioners but meant to also encompass people-driven leaders from all walks of life.

Let's take a closer look at this foundational framework by exploring each of the five segments—Purpose, Passion, People, Possibility, and Power—processing not only their full meaning, but also the call to action that accompanies each statement.

Purpose

> *I am a Human Resources Practitioner who helps individuals believe they have a purpose—both within our organizations and in life.*

It is when we openly accept that we have a purpose that the first traces of inner harmony can be experienced. This purpose reiterates that we were destined for much more than paperwork and party planning. Human Resources as a profession was meant to serve a greater good within organizations. More importantly, it is a purpose that establishes value that no longer needs to be pieced together with half-hearted arguments, knowing that our reason for existence is to support the true heart of the organization. A true acknowledgment of purpose allows us to put to rest the doubt of our worthiness and begin to focus our energies on being present in the work we were always meant to do.

I remember once seeing a social media post that said something like, "Not everyone has a purpose. Some of us are simply wanderers." This concept baffled me, especially when you think about what it means to be a wanderer. To aimlessly wander is to live with little or no intention. Life becomes about two basic things: birth and death, with possibly a few cool experiences in between. Perhaps we need to revisit the idea of purpose, because I don't want you to associate purpose with a grand goal or destination. Life is very much a journey and purpose is about living it intentionally.

Purpose is about knowing that you play a part in a much bigger picture of the world. Your everyday actions generate ripples that impact and influence others. I have come to believe that because many have decided to ignore this responsibility, the absence of their much needed ripples have now caused the suffering we experience in the world today. *Yes!* I believe the suffering is a direct result of someone not showing up, refusing to believe that they too needed to answer the question of why they are here. *Why* is a fully loaded question that encompasses a small dose of personal satisfaction and a mammoth amount of how you are changing the world. *Yes!* Changing the world—a goal normally reserved for super heroes is in actuality a goal for us all. It is the collective of purpose-driven energies that can shift the world's active dynamics.

It is when we live and work in alignment with our purpose that we create a harmonious environment for ourselves. We begin to operate more so as a conduit to the work that is needed and find that it occurs naturally with little resistance on our end. We find that this path embodies the highest level of integrity we hold dear.

Passion

I am a Human Resources Practitioner who helps individuals find their passion, and then I help them find ways to keep that fire burning brightly.

Passion and fire are truly one in the same. Now when I think of Passion, I cannot help but think of the fire-making challenges used for tie breakers in the popular reality TV show, *Survivor*. The amount of practice and skill it takes to create fire at will in nature is an art. Passion is no different. Our passion is not sustainable unless we tend to it. Yet, we can only tend to it if we have the right skills.

The lessons to sustain passion come from the greatest fire of all, the fire that is within. This fire resides dormant in the heart until triggered.

Take a moment and think about your most passionate moments. What did your body physically experience during the event? If you were able to pause and check-in during that moment you'd more than likely describe it as the rising of heat in your body. Specifically, more like a warmth that begins in the center of the chest and gradually builds toward the brain. Once the warmth rises to the top of the head, you may have even begun to feel a bit lightheaded or even spacey. This is the wave of passion that we experience countless times throughout our lives. For most of us the passion is spontaneous and unsustainable. We are at its mercy, either longing for or fully immersed in its presence.

Passion was always intended to be a powerful energy, a force we use to make powerful change happen. It was never intended to be the guiding force that many have relied on it to become, thinking moments of passionate release are hints of a path to happiness. In fact, passionate releases are often a hint that we are not doing enough work within. The fire of the heart is tended by self-care—a kind of self-care that fully respects your entire being, a kind of self-care that recognizes your pure self. It is that recognition and respect that allows passion to transform into a creative energy, an energy that can be used to inspire change and provide resiliency to bring vision to fruition.

People

I am a Human Resources Practitioner who is devoted to people, recognizing that they are the number one asset of any organization. I also recognize they are people with a diversity that needs to be fostered.

For the last two years, I have struggled with being able to articulate a true definition of who a HRart worker is. Sure, the phrase itself is catchy but how do you know who is and who is not a HRart worker? What I have discovered is that people are the non-negotiable qualifier in identifying a HRart worker.

People must be a primary driving force. This includes being a driving force of irritation. Regardless, what matters here is that the presence of people is a necessity for these individuals. They know on some level, even if only subconsciously, that people are the game changer in all aspects of life, especially their own. Therefore, if I meet someone who legitimately has no interest or concern for the people in their life, they are not a HRart worker. These individuals are more concerned with focusing their energy on manifesting tangible items of value rather than being bothered by the unseen magic of human connections. It may seem simple, but isn't often the true starting point. People must be present in your vision for work and life. If not, I am going to guess that this book has been a struggle for you… and to be honest, I am surprised you've made it to Chapter Four.

In graduate school, one of my professors shared a story about work she had done with an organization while on sabbatical. She was attempting to integrate artistic methods with organizational development work and had tasked a leadership team to collage a board of images representing their vision for the organization. My professor was amazed when she saw boards created by leaders that had not one person on it represented, instead they included images of graphs, charts, and references to money. It became clear to her in that moment that the struggles they were experiencing culturally were rooted in people not being part of the vision.

For HRart workers, people have a powerful presence. Not only can we recognize the potential they play in achieving mission and vision for organizations, we also recognize that they deliver the most impactful growth lessons for ourselves. People are a source of true mental clarity. They guide us into uncharted facets of ourselves. Expanding our horizons and blazing open new doors confidently and often unknowingly. Our growth often occurs amidst their own learning as we become intertwined as the true HRart workers we are.

Possibility

I am a Human Resources Practitioner who believes in possibilities, in dreams, in visions, and in our ability to make them happen.

I briefly mentioned *vision* in our discussion on people, but it is at the core when talking about possibility. The genuine belief that an organization's vision is absolutely possible to obtain someday is essential for a HRart worker. It is in this realm of chance that our resiliency is strengthened that fuels our consistent pursuit.

However it is important to note that to sustain our capacity to believe in this realm, we must possess courage—courage to not succumb to the doubt and skepticism we encounter on a consistent basis. It is important to recognize that this belief in possibility enables you to see the world and how it works with a level of transparency that others cannot comprehend. You are able to *know*—and I use that word intentionally—to embody the deep trust you possess for your intuition because you will know how we all connect together. You will *know* with clear sight that is sometimes accompanied with achingly beautiful details of how it will all one day materialize if we stay the course... if we trust.

That is what makes possibility so difficult to sustain. It is the one quality that is initially so easily obtained. It provides the source of inspiration that motivates us to pursue this work with dreams of being an agent of change in the world and it slowly transforms into hope. Our belief eventually fades, hoping change is coming but instead of leading we simply try to survive. But if we are not leading, we are hindering our ability to truly serve in manifesting what's possible.

We must find a way to remain in the realm of chance, navigating our work through the lens of transparency. We must possess a sense of acceptance for the fact that others will not initially see or believe like we do, but know that over time our work will enable them to do so. Therefore, this path of possibility is not for the faint of HRart, it is for those willing to commit. The commitment demanded is not solely to believe but to ensure that you are able to believe. This often requires us to revisit how we live, to identify practices that were initiated because possibility was transforming into hoping. In ways, hope is that final act of desperation before giving up completely.

Where are you on the path of possibility? Are you believing or hoping?

Power

I am a Human Resources Practitioner who believes in power—an empowerment so strong and true that individuals bring their authentic voice to our organizations being aligned with our vision and values.

The power we possess comes when we can remove our ego's reaction to an act and fully view it from intention. In my book, *From Heart to HRart*, I share the first time I experienced this skill and despite how "un-normal" it seemed. Internally all I could feel was an intense vibration of connectedness to my path. I wonder what it would be like to experience that sensation free-flowing throughout the day, being the only source of reaction to the things we encounter in our daily lives.

It is this power that enables us to create strategies and remain resilient in our work. Flawed strategies and our desire to disengage predominantly originate from a collective of ego-based reactions to acts we encounter. These ego-based reactions commonly begin with emotion. Emotions are important for fully experiencing an event in our lives but it is our tendency to want to hold on to them and revisit them incessantly that makes it unhealthy.

This power enables us to see the unseen, to see the intricate way all of our paths are woven together, and the power potential we have as a community functioning from a place of connectedness. A HRart worker works diligently to not only strengthen this power but also empowers its ability to awaken in others.

It is at this level, when the five Ps combine, that we are able to finally have the impact we were always meant to have as people-driven leaders. It is in this space that the missing element from our cultures is finally found and organizational loyalty can be restored. It is here, where we stop using buzzwords to diagnose our cultures and begin focusing on the humanness, that is the ingredient for organizational greatness.

Why Are You Here?

For nearly a decade I have facilitated leadership development using a methodology that integrates reflective practice and play. The outcomes for those who complete the curriculum range on a scale of satisfied to game changing. Yet, despite these successes I couldn't ignore the small number of individuals who did not complete the curriculum and would randomly disappear during our time together. A few years ago I decided to follow my curiosity and discover where these people went and why didn't they finish. The answer was that they each discovered while looking within that they were not called to be leaders. They recognized their vision was not people-driven and decided to move on. Yes, they moved on, transitioning to other positions, industries and some even retired early.

I believe that we are not asking the *why* question enough to leaders. We certainly are not asking *why* enough to HR practitioners. The professional capacity that HRart workers fill will always require more than monotonous actions. We are gifted with the privilege of seeing and unleashing potential. We are challenged to navigate the diverse humanness that changes the world. We help those that cannot yet understand, take baby steps towards believing.

Therefore, I now ask you the most important question of your career.

Why are you here?

PART TWO

THE MOURNING DOVE
ASKS US TO
CLEANSE AND CULTIVATE

CHAPTER FIVE

THE GHOSTS OF WORKPLACES PAST

We must undo what has been done, the molding that has been sculpted by those who are not called to serve in HR.

I believe many of us underestimate the doings of past workplaces. To call them ghosts is no exaggeration. These experiences I am referencing truly do haunt us. It is also these same experiences that we suppress and hold onto tightly, viewing the pain and struggle as a badge of honor.

They made us stronger, wiser, and more resilient... right? Actually they made us evolve into an individual who is afraid, uncertain, and numb. Depending on how many of these experiences you have cataloged in your system, it could be causing the worst outcome yet—ultimate disengagement. This is disengagement beyond work; it is disengagement of life.

This is where the myth of the necessary line between work and life truly sabotages us, our trained thought pathway to sever any connection leads us to doubt that the two can ever really impact each other. When in fact, inevitably the two are woven together in a beautiful, unique dance that is only your own.

The threads of passion are different within each of us, and it is for this reason that the methodology for undoing what has been done cannot be articulated lightly. It will require a journey of discomfort, venturing down a path you'd much rather not revisit. It means examining these paths through a transparent lens, vacant of all the conclusions you have possessed for so long.

We are about to embark together on a vulnerable conquest to visit your ghosts of workplaces past, present, and future. To do this we must begin with an exercise that trains and opens your mind's eye— or what many refer to as your *third eye*. It is this eye located in the center of your forehead that allows you to see the unseen. It is this eye that will navigate visits with each of your ghostly encounters, so if you rarely partake in viewing through your mind's eye, the necessary lessons will be unable to present themselves. Therefore, we shall begin with a little mind's eye warm-up.

Mind's Eye Warm-Up

This exercise will potentially materialize in various ways for you. There truly is no way to predict which way it will manifest, but you can at least anticipate one of the following completely normal responses:

1. You will see and feel nothing. If this is what you experience, this road will be challenging and patience will be necessary. You must trust that with each time you practice the exercise you are awakening and the desired outcome will indeed materialize. However, it will take time and if you attempt to rush this process your outcomes will lack the luster you seek. It also means you can expect more time. Your journey will be slower as we gradually tackle each task at your personal speed. Give yourself permission to pause right here with this exercise for as long as it takes, knowing the following pages await your return when you are ready.

2. You kinda see something or feel something. Here is what I need you to hear: Just because you kinda got something from the exercise does not mean you mastered it. The kinda experience is not the green light to move forward. Take your time and complete this warm-up exercise multiple times until *kinda* transforms into *knowing*. You should know exactly what you see or feel. It is this sense of knowing that signals that you are ready to proceed to your first ghostly encounter.

3. You see and feel and can describe it easily with detail. This does happen on the first try for some people, even for those who rarely participate in visualization exercises. Don't question it; simply embrace it. The greatest resistance I commonly see with this materialization is doubt that what they experienced was "it"—convincing themselves that they had to have done something wrong. You did nothing wrong. What you saw and felt were exactly it.

This exercise is made up of two steps, however each one is hefty and therefore we will take a moment to delve into them separately. I cannot reiterate enough, do not move on from step one until you are able to complete it comfortably—meaning with a complete absence of frustration, irritation, and restlessness.

Step One: Respect the Monkey Mind

In order to open the mind's eye, it is necessary to first quiet the monkey mind—the endless roaming thoughts of things to do, what-if scenario processing and our desire to always remain in control. To do this, the act is simple. It requires finding a place where you can settle in and not be disturbed, closing your eyes and paying attention.

Initially anticipate needing this space for a minimum of 10-15 minutes, however as you become familiar with the exercise and progress toward its completion, you will find yourself practicing with ease for 5-minute durations in the most bizarre places, like in line at the grocery store or in front of the TV as your family is immersed in their latest Netflix binge. But a safe, protected space is where you must begin.

Respecting the monkey mind is a requirement. This mind serves us greatly as it triggers survival skills. For the majority of our life it has been successful in its one major task of protection, yet in this moment we now need to revisit all the times when the monkey mind believed it was doing what was best. We understand that sometimes its quick reaction of generating fear is meant to deter us, and that may have created unnecessary limitations, but a life without the monkey mind is not possible. We are not attempting to shut it down or make it disappear. We are more so asking it to step aside for a moment, acknowledging and providing the necessary gratitude for all it has done while clearly articulating that we expect and value its presence always.

Let's begin...

1. Settle into your seat, ensuring you are comfortable. If this means lying down, then by all means please do so.

2. Close your eyes and begin to notice your breath with the goal of not controlling or transforming it but rather noticing the subtleties. Allow the breath to bring you further within by feeling every sensation, the warmth and coolness, the rise and fall of the body, the expansiveness and contracting within.

3. Now begin to notice and take stock of your internal distractions—thoughts that are swirling around, feelings that want to rise to the surface, or even physical sensations of discomfort. Notice them all, asking each one to present itself individually so you may fully acknowledge it. Imagining these thoughts, feelings, and sensations lining up in order of urgency, ready to be seen.

4. As each thought, feeling, and sensation presents itself, recognize it for what it is, with no expectation of resolving it but just instilling a knowing of its presence. In recognition of its presence, ask if this thought, feeling, or sensation is willing to step aside so others may be seen. Assure it that you will return soon and that there is no intention for this acknowledgment and action to serve as resolution.

5. Continue this process until all thoughts, feelings, and sensations that desire to be seen have been seen. It is when you stand in the presence of nothingness that you may proceed to Step Two. It is important to note that not all your

thoughts, feelings, and sensations will want to be seen. Some will willingly step aside as you engage in this exercise without needing that spotlight moment. Therefore it is natural for your line-up to adjust in length, partially due to the fact that most of our thoughts, feelings, and sensations are linked in a domino-like fashion, with the first domino being the most pressing circumstance to be witnessed.

Step Two: Where-Am-I Land

As you proceed to Step Two, remember to trust yourself, trust what you see, what you feel, and what you embrace. If you choose to surrender during this step and immerse yourself, your mind's eye will flood open ready to serve as you continue your healing work.

This step begins after you have completed actions 1-5 to quiet the monkey mind.

6. Once all thoughts, feelings, and sensations have respectfully moved to the side, you will find yourself in a state of stillness, a true state of nothingness. Sit with this presence of no expectations, no real sensations of any kind, a literal place of peace.

7. Allow your breath to guide you deeper into this state, making each inhale longer and deeper, allowing the exhale to match in duration and depth.

8. When you feel well established in the state of nothingness, ask the stillness one question. "Where am I?"

9. Allow your mind's eye to create an image of your surroundings, complete with the most vivid details. This may materialize initially as only a single detail that you can focus on while everything else remains a blur. Embrace that single image; immerse yourself in it, exploring every inch and opening your mind even further to all the accompanying characteristics. What are you feeling, thinking, knowing in that moment as you take it in? If an entire scene has materialized for you, explore, taking in as much as possible.

But do not rush! Take your time, approaching each element with a genuine curiosity, a desire to know what it has to share with you.

10. When you feel like it is time to conclude your visit, bring your attention back to your breath, allowing the scene to dissipate, placing you back in the nothingness. Slowly return your breath to normal as you begin to awaken your body. Moving your fingers, toes, and even your head gently from side to side. Then when you are ready, open your eyes.

What Does It Mean?

What you saw and felt will be different for everyone. I use this exercise frequently with clients in order to open their mind's eye and awaken the guidance they possess within. During our coaching sessions, I am always amazed to hear what they saw and felt as each person shares the intricate details of their experience.

Personally, I see a beautiful garden on a cliff overlooking the ocean. It is filled with big, vibrant, beautiful purple and blue flowers. On my first visit, I spent the whole time just taking in this violet flower, smelling it and touching it, experiencing it fully. I can hear the waves crashing below and the sky always seems to be paused on the most beautiful sunset at the horizon, with hints of the moonlit night peeking through. There are children playing, I hear their laughter and see them running on the fresh green lawn. I can feel my bare feet on the grass with the smell of a newly mowed lawn always in the air. There's an adorable red accented patio set on the lawn in the direction of a lighthouse that can be seen in the backdrop, it has two chairs and a small table with an umbrella. There is always a visitor, who is never the same. Every visit, I never leave the garden, I never venture to the cliff's edge or desire to head toward the lighthouse. I am always perfectly content being immersed in the garden, the laughter, and the time with my visitor.

That is what I see, but I didn't even begin to share what I feel and think about. This is a place I can only describe to you as your soul's home. It is where you are most connected and most clear. It is where you are the most you, once all the layers of external influencers are moved aside. This place was originally intended to be where we go to contemplate and decide our paths moving forward, rather than making decisions with strictly our ego. It is here where we can separate the levels of fear, knowing which can cause us harm and which are limiting us.

As we move forward, it is important to remember this place and know that you can return to it at any time. I actually encourage you to do so as frequently as you feel innately called. This place will serve as neutral ground as you begin to sort through the haunting experiences of your past. It will also serve you greatly as you navigate your daily life. I have clients who use this place when they experience overwhelm or disconnection during their day, returning for only a few minutes to recenter and make decisions that serve their highest good.

Now that you have a home base, we may begin our healing work… and that work must start at the root.

Which Ghost Visits First

Remember the domino visual image from the previous exercise? Essentially that is the same protocol here. The ghost that you will visit first from your past is the first domino. When I first mentioned that we would be exploring your past work lives, it is understandable that the task may have felt daunting. Especially if you've been working for a while, but what is important to keep in mind is when we refuse to learn a lesson that is instrumental in moving us forward, the lesson presents itself over and over and more intensely. Therefore, it is likely there is not a true ghost for every place you have worked, but rather there is one that has revisited in different manifestations at other times.

To determine your first ghost, it should be pretty easy. It is typically the work situation that is the oldest and you still talk about on a fairly regular basis. This ghost often rises to the surface and so you find yourself sharing that work situation in a venting fashion over and over. If you can't think of one, ask a venting buddy, someone whom you would commonly gush to. Ask them what is the workplace, work situation, boss, that comes up consistently. If you try this and are still bewildered, then you'll just have to do it the old-fashioned way and begin with job *numero uno*. Yes, your first job ever, like your first job. For me, I was a snack bar girl at the local ice arena.

Your First Visit

Are you ready? Of course you're not—no one is ever really ready to revisit a haunting past, but I think instinctively you know it is necessary. The process to visit these ghosts of workplaces past follows a similar process to our mind's eye warm-up. Think of the warm-up as your training wheels and now you're ready to ride without them. If you don't feel confident enough to proceed on your own, feel free to return to the warm-up exercise.

To visit your first ghost you must first successfully quiet the monkey mind (actions 1-5 of the warm-up). Once you are in the state of nothingness, proceed by doing the following:

1. Allow your mind to wander, remembering the workplace of the past you'd like to revisit. Then ask, "Where was I?"

2. As your mind begins to materialize visual imagery, fully take stock of everything you are experiencing, particularly any physical sensations or emotions in the body.

3. Recognize your emotions and physical sensations as a separate element of the visit and focus on what you visually are able to observe. Where and when are you? Is it a particular memory replaying? Are certain individuals around you? Are you in a specific location of your workplace? Are you unable to answer any of those questions because you are strictly focused on one thing? What is that one thing?

4. Make a mental note of all of your observations and curiosities. Make sure to mentally log your emotions,

random thoughts, and physical sensations in the body. Where is the emotion living?

5. Once you feel your visit is complete, you can begin to allow the imagery and accompanying elements to dissipate, returning back to the state of nothingness. Then begin the process of slowly waking up your body as we did at the conclusion of the warm-up.

Immediately after your visit, pour your mental visit log onto paper. Allow the words to flow freely, do not worry about spelling or sentence structure, just capturing as much as possible while it freshly sits in front of the mind. After your notes are captured, move right into a reflection, capturing your reaction to all or one of the following prompts. Write only for a few minutes.

- What are you thinking right now?

- What are you feeling right now?

- What do you need right now?

- What do you want right now?

Your Next Visit and Visits After

The next visit can once again be determined by only you. You must trust yourself as to what is next. This could mean revisiting the first workplace once again. It could mean moving on to another workplace or the literal second workplace of your life. The only thing I need you to hear is that visiting these ghosts of the past are necessary and must be revisited before we move on to the ghosts of present and future. In fact, the past provides the healing framework for you to address the ghosts of present and future. Therefore, do not rush this. Continue the visit exercise as many times as needed. You will know when you have completed this task and it is time to move forward.

In the next chapter, we will begin to explore healing what you have uncovered so far. You have my permission to read on just a little bit more to acquire the tools to begin the healing process. You will find that releasing while revisiting is a very complimentary practice.

Chapter Six

The Present with Breath

"If my environment dictates my mood, then my life will feel like a roller coaster. The way to steady ground is through my   breath."
– Gabrielle Bernstein

When it comes to visiting the ghosts of our current workplace, the practice of visiting the past will seem like a walk in the park. It is always easier to look back and possibly acknowledge that there is something left to learn from that experience. However, when you are experiencing the moment for the first time it is extremely difficult to step away to observe, take in and embrace curiosity while emotions and defense mechanisms are heightened. Your breath will become the most powerful tool to complete this next visit. It will also serve as a great releasing tool for all that you have uncovered that does not serve you.

Therefore, before we begin even discussing the second visit, we will utilize the breath releasing work as our warm-up this round.

The Breath

Breathing is the most basic practice of Qigong. *Qi*, meaning life force or energy, and *gong*, meaning gather or work. Qigong is simply a practice of working and caring for our energy, the force that allows us to be alive as the unique beings we are. When we breathe in air, we inhale new, nourishing energy. When we breathe out, we exhale what does not serve us. Regardless of whether you are intentionally guiding this act, it occurs naturally, organically cleansing and cultivating our energy. Yet with lack of intention, this breath cycle focuses on survival rather than actively clearing toxins or turbid Qi buildup from the system. In Chinese Medicine, it is believed that the accumulation of turbid Qi in our energetic bodies, if left unaddressed, begins to materialize as physical disease. It is then that our physical bodies begin the work of protecting us, for example, the functions of the liver.

> "Truth is, your liver is the best friend you've ever had. It performs over 2,000 critical functions that are undiscovered by medical research and science. It works hard for you night and day. It prepares ahead when it knows you need extra support, and it's there to clean up the mess after your earthly mistakes. It's a storehouse, a filter, a processing center, a garbage service, and more. It shields you, it protects you, and it defends you from every angle. It's been looking out for you all along—putting out fires, defusing bombs, taking bullets for you, rounding up the bad guys inside of you, and preventing internal disasters. Your liver is the reason, after everything you've been through in life, that you're still alive." (William, A., *Liver Rescue*, 5)

But despite how hard our bodies work to care for us, they cannot undo all the harm we have caused. Physical cleanses and detoxes are trends embraced and encouraged by the wellness industry because they provide added support to our bodies, by encouraging and sometimes forcing the release of what does not serve us.

Through my studies and research of applying Chinese Medicine principles to professional development, I have come to believe that the root reason we become toxic is a lack of caring for our energetic systems. This negligence begins with a simple yet detrimental societal teaching to suppress emotions. In fact, most of us never do end up processing and releasing them because of another societal teaching surrounding mental health and therapy. But you do not need to relive the emotions to release them; you only need to breathe with intention.

Therapy and counseling is always helpful because it helps to unpack what gets unleashed as we explore our emotional reactions to circumstances. The mental health profession is an absolute necessity when working through suppressed severe trauma. Without question, certain emotional unpacking should not be done alone. If you find trauma of this nature being released through any part of this healing work, please seek out a mental health professional before continuing. But for the trauma that most of us experience as normal everyday life, breath will be of deep service.

Natural Breath

For our purposes, you will want to ensure that you are engaging in what is called *natural breath*. When you inhale, fill the abdominal cavity. As a result, the belly rises. As you exhale you empty the abdominal cavity causing the belly to fall.

Take a moment to check if this form of breathing is in fact your natural breath. To do so, place your hands on your belly and notice when they rise and fall in correlation with the breath. You may find that reverse breathing is your innate breathing pattern, which is when the belly falls on inhale and rises on exhale. If this is the case, you will need to practice the natural breath method before engaging in the releasing exercise.

Use the following three steps to practice natural breathing:

1. Place your hands on your belly and inhale for five counts, feeling the belly rise.

2. Pause and hold the breath for five counts. The belly should be expanded.

3. Begin to exhale for five counts, feeling the belly fall.

Repeat this practice until the breath pattern is comfortable.

Releasing What Does Not Serve Me

This breath practice will include two evolutions. The first is to solely add intention to your practice. Your intention directs how each inhale and exhale will serve you. The intention for this practice is merely to release what does not serve you from your healing work. Recognize that with every ghost of the workplace past you revisited, you unleashed wisdom but also suppressed emotion.

Emotions serve us greatly in the moment as they are a primary mode of communication from our soul. They also are a survival mechanism that protects us from actual harm. However, when we revisit a moment and receive the accompanying emotions of that time, they are simply another element to be curious about. But since our typical reaction in those moments is to suppress uncomfortable emotions coupled with the lack of any future processing, this can create the potential resurrection of an emotional storm that must be cleared. This is the vision behind your intention for the breath practice: to clear the storm, to be able to see that blue sky of transparency so you can soak up all the wisdom it has to offer.

Let's begin...

1. Close your eyes and begin natural breathing using your nose. The inhale and exhale should both occur through the nostrils.

2. Begin slowing the inhale, pausing for a moment when the breath is full, and then slowly exhaling. Attempt to match the duration of the exhale to that of the inhale.

3. Continue deepening the inhale and exhale, providing permission for the mind to wander to a place of nothingness.

4. Once there, inhale through the nostrils while silently saying, *I breathe in healing energy. Restore me and serve my highest good.*

5. Exhale through the mouth, while silently saying, *I release all that does not serve me.*

Repeat steps four and five until you feel complete, and then feel free to begin waking up your body from the exercise. You may experience a physical emotional release such as tears or strong sensations of anger or sadness. It is important that if these arise to keep breathing and not stop the practice; this is merely the passing of strong rooted emotions dragging themselves out of the body.

Also, feel free to sigh if it feels natural on the exhale. Always remembering that the exhale is serving as a release. It is the pathway for the exit so if it serves you to sigh, or to have a longer, quicker or more intense exhale, please do so. The inhale should feel warm and compassionate, while the exhale should leave you feeling cool and lighter.

The Second Evolution

The second evolution of this breath practice involves magnifying the intention by directly targeting the emotion that is surfacing. As you have engaged in your visits to the ghosts of workplaces past emotions have emerged. The feelings you are experiencing are rooted in one of five core emotions. To engage in this next level of releasing breathwork, you must identify which core emotion or emotions is bubbling to the surface.

The five core emotions are:

1. Grief: This includes any form of sadness.

2. Anger: This includes frustration, irritation, jealousy, and animosity.

3. Anxiety: This includes deep-rooted emotions felt in the heart area as well as excessive spouts of uncontrollable passion.

4. Doubt: This includes doubt of self and questioning of worthiness or a general lack of self-confidence.

5. Fear: This encompasses all fears, including those related to the future and failure.

In Medical Qigong, each emotion has a healing sound associated with it. When this sound is used, it deepens the release. For our purposes, we will simply use the sounds inaudibly, transforming your previous exhaled sigh to one with a specific sound formation.

The sounds that accompany each core emotion are:

Grief	*shhh, sss*
Anger	*shu (shoo)*
Anxiety	*haa*
Doubt	*whooo, hooo*
Fear	*yuuu (you)*

You will notice that certain core emotions have multiple sounds. These may be used interchangeably during your practice. Inevitably you will find that one sound sensationally serves you greater than another. This will also change as your practice continues, so always ensure you are tuning in. However, if you check out and continue using the same sound, don't worry that it will become ineffective— it will still be productive, but it merely will not be the most effective.

To use the sound, begin this evolution of breath practice the same way as the last. Steps 1-4 are exactly the same. It is in step 5 that you will incorporate the sound.

Let's begin...

1. Close your eyes and begin natural breathing using your nose.

2. Begin slowing the inhale, pausing for a moment when the breath is full, and then slowly exhaling.

3. Continue deepening the inhale and exhale, wandering to a place of nothingness.

4. Once there, inhale through the nostrils while silently saying, *I breathe in healing energy. Restore me and serve my highest good.*

5. Exhale through the mouth, inaudibly sighing the sound associated with your identified core emotion. (Ex: If you identified anxiety, you would exhale while silently sighing on a "*haaa*" sound.)

Repeat steps 4-5 until you feel complete and then begin waking up your body from the exercise. The entire act should sound breathy in the outside world but send powerful vibrations within. You may progress through your practice incorporating other core emotion sounds. Do not feel pressured to only clear one emotion per practice. If you identified more than one emotion, feel free to listen to your inner guidance and work on releasing them all or focus solely on one. This is your practice, so tune into what your body and soul are asking for.

The Emotional Key to the Present

The core emotions that have surfaced during your journeys to visit ghosts of the workplace past provides the path markers for your way forward. In order to visit the ghosts of the present workplace you must first find where these emotions live and then discover when they are occurring and what causes them. It is through this process that you will uncover all you need to know to clear at this stage and continue cultivating your healing journey.

To prepare for your visit with these second ghosts—yes, I intentionally use the plural—we need to engage in yet another warm-up. This exercise will deepen your inner attunement, proving powerful as we progress together. You should expect to visit multiple ghosts during this second clearing stage. Despite the fact that you work for one place of employment, this dynamic environment is full of triggers that have been feeding and building on the stories started by workplaces past. It is here in the now that we can easily dismiss opportunities to learn and grow because our evolved defensive mechanism deters us at rapid fire. Logically it makes sense—why waste time reacting or processing events that resemble even vaguely a past experience that caused us internal turmoil? But it is these rash assumptions, driven by a belief that we know what's best, that results in complete backfire. It is often here in this stage that I find individuals literally stuck. They have found a comfortable hamster wheel, that perhaps they initially ran on but have now slowed on with multiple breaks… because honestly what's the point?

Where Do They Live

You will need to complete this warm-up exercise with any primary core emotions that have arisen, in other words, any emotion you found yourself feeling time and again as a result of your previous workplace encounters. Ideally, this would include emotions associated with the sounds you utilized during the breath release exercises. Have a journal and writing implement nearby. You will need them immediately upon completing this exercise.

Pick one of these primary core emotions and let's begin…

1. Close your eyes and begin natural breathing using your nose.

2. Begin slowing the inhale, pausing for a moment when the breath is full, and then slowly exhaling.

3. Continue deepening the inhale and exhale, wandering to a place of nothingness.

4. Now begin to focus your attention on the primary core emotion you identified. (Ex: If you chose fear, you will focus your attention on the feeling of fear.)

5. Become curious about what has caused this emotion in the past. (Ex: With fear, you might ask your mind, "What have I been afraid of? What has caused me fear in the past? What am I afraid of now as a result?")

6. Allow the mind's eye to populate imagery, sensations, and thoughts that provide responses to these prompts. With each new entry, provide permission for your body to experience the emotion, intensifying the physical sensations.

7. Once the emotions have reached a level of intensity that is enough for you, release the images, sensations, and thoughts—holding onto only the physical sensations of the emotion.

8. Imagine compressing the physical sensation into a compact ball of emotion. Compress it to a point where you could hold it in your hands if you wanted to.

9. Ask now, "Where does this compact ball live? Physically in the body where does this compact ball of compressed intense emotion live? What does it physically feel like?"

10. Mentally log what you are feeling and observing.

11. You may now begin to release the ball of emotion, allowing the physical sensations and core emotion to dissipate in intensity and return to the present moment.

12. When you begin to feel grounded again, wake your body from the exercise.

Immediately after you open your eyes, grab your pen or pencil and write. Capture what you logged in your mind regarding where the emotion lives in your body and how you physically experience it.

You will eventually be invited to return to this warm-up exercise to reveal the physical living space of other core emotions that have surfaced. However, I'd like you to move forward with your first visit to the ghost of the present workplace before unlocking more emotions. It will be easier to conduct this visit if you are solely focused on one emotion. Remember, these emotions are your guide for present visits so it's best to have only one screaming at you the first time!

Visiting a Ghost of the Present Workplace

The challenge for this visit comes in the form of divine timing. Despite whatever your belief system, the gist is that you do not get to decide when or where this visit occurs. The visit will occur in the time and space where a lesson is to be learned. Your only task is to remain present and aware.

The signal for when the lesson is occurring will materialize as a triggered core emotion. However, you will not be seeking the emotion but rather the physical sensation of how the emotion comes alive in your body, specifically being activated where you now know it lives in your body.

For example, when I processed my past work lives, the primary core emotion that bubbled to the surface was fear. To be fully transparent, it was fear of being alone. I had a deep fear that I was always destined to be alone. The encounters from my past workplaces that fed this fear were moments when I felt completely unseen and practically invisible to my work counterparts. Upon discovering where this fear lived in my body, I found myself experiencing panic-like symptoms in the center of my chest. When this fear was activated, it was like the world was closing in and spinning fast. Recognizing this physical sensation as fear allowed me to discover how it was materializing in my daily work.

I completed my first round of present workplace visits during the start of my entrepreneurial journey. My fear was heightened because I began the journey alone and, to no surprise, immediately became obsessed about when I could hire another person and create a team. What I discovered was that my fear's physical sensations activated in so many situations, the sensations were not always as intense as past encounters or when I completed the Where Do They Live discovery exercise, but even the subtle hints of sensations were always blatantly obvious as fear. This fear dictated how I entered networking spaces, new client proposals, strategic planning for my business and even hiring decisions when I did begin building a team.

I share this to illustrate that your present workplace visits will not be accompanied with the intense sensations you experienced in the discovery exercise. If you do find yourself experiencing that type of magnified visit, it's likely because you have been distracted, missing the subtle but still clear signals, resulting in a massive lesson. Our lessons build, especially when we provide permission to our soul to finally speak!

Don't make this visit more complicated than it is. If you find yourself pausing in a moment and asking, "What is that I'm feeling?" I guarantee it's a core emotion activating. Feel it and then question it. *What is triggering that emotion in this moment? What do you need to learn right now to serve your highest good?* Make sure to write it down as soon as possible. In fact, if you've been using a journal to log your findings throughout this process, take it with you to work so it is easily accessible and you can keep all your logs in one place.

The present visits are the only ones you cannot control for frequency and quantity. Therefore, when you've had enough, simply set the intention for the visits to stop. Sounds easy, but it's effective, especially since it was strictly your initial intention that made them begin.

Make no mistakes… you will return to engage in more visits in the future. It is when we can learn in the present space that we truly become powerful. As healers, we are always learning and therefore present-day lessons will keep coming, pushing us to continually raise our vibration and evolve to yet another greater version of ourselves.

CHAPTER SEVEN

INNER CHILD ASPIRATIONS

"To my abusers: I went back and healed that younger part of me that you wounded, and per their request you are no longer welcome here." —Nate Postlethwait

This quote caught my attention on Instagram as a result of following #empath. Nate is a survivor who shares his thoughts on healing trauma and is an inner child work advocate. He is the founder of Inner Child Chats, a safe space for survivors to connect with their inner child. As I clicked on the @inner_child_chats handle, I was overwhelmed by images of children and their accompanying stories. Each picture was an actual image of an inner child with a story told by the adult that now lives today. The ages varied from all walks of childhood starting at as young as two. These amazing individuals are doing the hard healing work to release their inner child, providing a safe space for that child to be free, able to experience joy and dream.

We all have experienced events of oppression, a moment in time when the ability to truly dream became limited. We were forced to become reasonable. Dreams were given requirements and certain expectations. For some it came way too early, accompanied with horrific trauma, events that many suppress so deeply they are completely unaware they are part of this healing journey.

I have found through my work as a master trainer and facilitator and my Medical Qigong studies that the inner child plays a critical role in our ability to move forward. It is the inner child who provides the true permission to play and experience life with an indescribable joy. It is the inner child who unleashes the wildest dreams of what you are truly able to make possible. But working with this inner child requires transparency and opening to memories that might have once been lost. I want to assure you that even if those memories are dark, holding onto them is silent destruction from within. There are so many resources and support available to do that hard healing work for your inner child who is terrified. I promise that even though the work is hard and ugly it will be so worth it on the other side. Please refer to the HR Healer Toolkit for recommendations of support should you experience a release of childhood trauma.

What Do You Want to Be When You Grow Up

For the majority of us, our professional paths are created by others. We are taught to embrace new opportunities, be excited about new doors when they open, and run through them with minimal hesitation. This is how we achieve titles of accomplishment that paint the picture of what our society dictates traditionally as success. However, this method of moving forward is similar to aimlessly wandering. Our intention is broad of merely aiming to achieve success as defined culturally. For me, this translates to a surface level success, which is the type of success I believe is most frequently experienced. It might be exciting in the moment but quickly turns into a feeding source for the ego that gobbles it up and wants more. That greedy ego is never satisfied.

An ego-driven path means choosing to work in super comfort, I'm-a-bum mode. Doesn't sound too bad—for me, this mode translates to sweatpants, binging Netflix and mindlessly snacking. The ego-driven path is a treat every once in a while but you would not want it incessantly. This mode translates to average work with no real impact or value, and eventually becomes the bare minimum to sustain employment. To some it may sound like heaven, but to me it's boring and life sucking, absent of joy or true connection.

As a child, we began to imagine adulthood, dreaming of the day when we could live our lives any way we wanted, a day when we would have freedom to choose how to live each and every day.

These fantasies don't often include "bum" mode. They are filled with visions of being teachers, musicians, scientists, or the President. These visions over the years become more "realistic" as we learn from our external environment that the concept of unlimited possibilities is unreasonable. But the original fantasies—the ones that we played time and time again—reemerged for a reason. They fed our soul, giving it a spark, one that would generate a warmth within. Yet we let those visions die, telling ourselves the soul's spark was unreasonable and impossible.

The Soul's Spark

It's time to remember those visions and reconnect to that spark, unleashing the feeling that once felt so good. This visit to your lost spark serves as the final ghost visit, the one of the future. The spark provides the initial whisper of what is truly possible for you and it does so by sharing with you the guiding feeling.

For this visit, you will want to find a place to settle in and not be disturbed for 15-30 minutes. Give yourself the space and time; you will not want to rush this visit. Past experience has shown me the first time you do this exercise is always the most powerful, so make sure you are able to give yourself permission to soak it all up.

Let's begin...

1. Settle into your seat, ensuring you are comfortable. If this means lying down, then by all means please do so.

2. Close your eyes and begin natural breathing using your nose. The inhale and exhale should both occur through the nostrils.

3. Begin slowing the inhale, pausing for a moment when the breath is full, and then slowly exhaling. Attempt to match the duration of the exhale to that of the inhale.

4. Continue deepening the inhale and exhale, providing permission for the mind to wander to a place of nothingness.

5. Once all thoughts, feelings, and sensations have respectfully moved to the side, you will find yourself in a state of stillness, with nothing but a chair. Sit in the chair with no expectations.

6. Take notice of a glass-like surface, now before you, that is slowly bringing forth an image of your reflection.

7. As the details formalize, see yourself clearly in front of you, a perfectly mirrored image of yourself sitting in a chair.

8. Move your gaze to the eyes of your reflection, aligning them to be perfectly matched. Allow yourself to become lost in the space between by going even deeper into your reflection's gaze.

9. Now begin to withdraw from the depths, backing out of your reflection's eyes so that you can see the outline of the face. This face no longer directly reflects your own but that of a younger version of yourself. As you continue retracting your gaze, now taking in the full image in front of you, you see the younger version of yourself has completely materialized and is present. Your younger self peers at you with the same bewilderment you are currently expressing on your face.

10. When ready, ask your younger self if they would like to go play. If they appear hesitant, assure them this is a safe place and that you genuinely want to play. Even if you feel yourself resisting that response, sit with it, stay there and be open to the opportunity for play.

11. Once your younger self agrees, say to yourself, *Let's play*. Allow your mind's eye to populate the perfect space to play and take in every detail. Follow your younger self's lead through the space, being open and curious.

12. As you immerse yourself in the play experience, take stock of how you feel, what physical sensations you are experiencing and where in the body you are experiencing

them. Take stock of what you are thinking about, making a mental log of each thought, no matter how random.

13. When you feel the time has come to say goodbye, let your younger self know. Take a moment to express your gratitude and love for your younger self and all that they have shared.

14. If it feels right, affirm to your younger self that you will return again and that you never want to forget what was shared in this space.

15. Start to bring your attention back to your breath, allowing your younger self to fade into the distance, placing you back in the nothingness. Slowly return your breath to normal and begin to awaken your body.

Immediately after your visit, pour your mental visit log onto paper. Allow the words to flow freely, while it freshly sits at the front of your mind. After your notes are captured, move right into exploring the sensations you experienced on a greater level.

The following prompts will guide you through this discovery:

- What physical sensations did you experience during the encounter?

- Where did the physical sensations reside in the body?

- When observing your thoughts, were there any themes or commonalities?

- When observing your thoughts, were there any that seemed extra random?

Searching for a Joy-Filled Sign

The physical sensations you experience in the Soul's Spark exercise serve as fuel for our final task in visiting the ghost of future workplaces. Because we have become so accustomed to believing we know what's best for ourselves at all times as adults, we have a tendency to turn a deaf ear to our soul.

I've already mentioned that the soul only attempts to share in moments of stillness; it refuses to fight with chaos. Yet it doesn't give up completely. It routinely puts out feelers to see if we are open, receptive, and available. The passive-aggressive method of choice is *signs*. Signs are random occurrences in life that generate an internal reaction often described as *dejavu*, or serendipity, oddly triggering or simply lingering weirdness. Signs also only make sense to you, therefore when I have attempted to explain my signs to another person I am always met with a good old smile and nod, disheartened that others cannot see the blazing neon sign I just identified. But other people's opinions or verifications of your signs are completely irrelevant. You and your interpretation is the only thing that matters, because this is a deep, intimate conversation between you and your soul, like love notes left by your special somebody.

The feeling you physically experienced in the Soul Spark exercise is reminiscent of a time when you freely connected with your soul and the feeling now is evidence of that. When we are connected, we feel that oh so good vibration from within, like we are tuned in perfect harmony with our intended path—a connected path that aligns with our greatest good, the path where we can be of greatest service to ourselves and others.

This exercise is a lot like your last visit to the ghosts of the workplace present, in that you cannot control it. You simply set an intention and then pay attention. One significant difference is that if you miss it, it will not magnify. This step is not only about receiving but also demonstrating that you are open, receptive, and available to some soul time. Take a moment and think about it... If your special somebody was leaving you love notes and you missed them because you weren't paying attention after you promised you would be, would they then work to create bigger, more grander notes? No, they would be pissed off and possibly stop all together. This is a two-way street, so you have to show up for your soul to continue speaking.

To begin, set an intention of *Show me my joy-filled signs*. Then pay attention for a ping or pings throughout the day, when something pipes up inside and says, "A Sign! A Sign!" Do not overthink or over-analyze. Is it really a sign? Yes, it is, so write it down. That is your only task right now... to capture it, feel the ping, and write it down.

What Does a Ping Feel Like?

A ping can feel like a short, intense burst of the sensation you experienced in the Soul's Spark exercise. A ping can feel like a light tingle reminding you of the sensation you experienced in the Soul's Spark. A ping can be any sensation you experience in your body at the same location where you experienced sensations in the Soul's Spark exercise. A ping can be nothing physically experienced but simply a strong knowing that this is a sign.

If it helps at all, my greatest joy-filled signs are animals, with the penguin and panda being at the forefront. They show up on random pieces of art, surprise zoo visits, random media appearances, and social media memes. Your joy-filled signs will find you!

CHAPTER EIGHT

STRENGTHENING YOUR INNATE NATURE

"Do you have the patience to wait till your mud settles and the water is clear? Can you remain unmoving till the right action arises by itself?" —Tao Te Ching

At this point, you have completed several visits that have opened your eyes in a new way. Whether you are looking back, forward, or here in the present moment, you can recognize a shift has occurred, even if you cannot adequately articulate what that shift is or what it means. As for what has literally transpired, all you have is a log filled with written observations from this journey and the beginning of potential conclusions but nothing concrete. You sit now in the muddy water, waiting for it to settle. Those of us who are filled with great passion are driven and ambitious, wanting to be the way-maker, courageously charging down the path. But to be of great service to your passion you must remain unmoving at times, waiting for the next right action. Or to quote a Disney troll from the *Frozen 2* movie, "When one can see no future, all one can do is the next right thing."

The Next Right Thing

What to do with all you have collected to this point is up to you. Only you can reveal the next right thing. Each of our paths are uniquely linked to our individuality, making them a guarantee that we have something to offer this world that no other can. It is for this reason that the guidance you desire regarding what to do with work you've done so far must be provided from within. However, since I know this art of looking inward is fairly new for you, I'll give you a few possible scenarios that could take shape.

A Theme Emerges

You may be guided to review your written log of observations from your visits to see what themes emerge. It is common to sometimes find that each visit was actually an evolution of others and speaks to one particular area for growth. These themes are often responses to one of the following prompts:

- What am I thinking about?

  Your thoughts are always sharing something with you and the thoughts that occur in spaces of intention are supreme in this capacity.

- What are you feeling?

  Feelings are your soul's words. Therefore do not dismiss them as a basic physical body reaction; they are so much more.

- What do you need?

  After all this work, with certainty, what do you know you need from this life or what do you need moving forward?

- What do you want?

  What great desire has your heart expressed? This may be a feeling and not something you can describe perfectly with words.

You're Not Done

As my sixth-grade math teacher, Ms. Porter, would say, "You're done? Well, then I'll stick a fork in you." Your next right thing might emerge as more visits are necessary. You might feel yourself pausing here and feeling called to return and repeat practices from previous chapters. This guidance should be heeded, because as you have been completing these exercises, you may have not been able yet to take a step back and realize what you have been actually accomplishing.

> *"Something lost.*
> *A part of yourself, perhaps.*
> *That which you seek*
> *inside you will find."*
> —*Yoda*

With each visit you have ventured inside and awoken a part of yourself that was maybe lost, but definitely under-utilized. You also provided permission through each exercise to remove the clutter of the mind and the limiting emotions to be able to begin seeing yourself with a genuine level of transparency—a transparency that delivers clarity without judgment, a mere recognition of who we are in this moment and how we got here; an acknowledgment that if we continue to choose the same, the path forward will possibly differ; a knowing that we can choose differently, intentionally, the possibilities that have always been waiting for us.

Let's be real. I'm still revisiting the ghosts of past, present, and future. This healing journey has no definitive deadline. In fact, I'm starting to believe this journey is endless. As we evolve, there will invariably be another lesson, likely one we were not capable of comprehending at the previous evolution. Embrace this invitation to return and continue.

You Just Know

This one causes a lot of unnecessary turmoil, because we are taught that things do not happen easily. However, when you are in alignment with your connected path, it does feel easy. Things seem to occur organically in their perfectly planned time and place. Yet behind this path is a lot of hard work—living in alignment once we have found our connected path is not easy. So do not confuse when things feel like they are just happening that you haven't been doing any work to make it happen. You have been working your tushy off! The exercises in the previous chapters are hard work so do not discount that. Know it is all a sign that you are on your connected path. What's next for you is figuring out how to stay there.

Living in Alignment

It's taken me nearly five years and over two dozen holistic practitioners to finally come to terms with the fact that there is no one path or way for us all to find—no yellow brick road that leads to the wizard of purpose. There is a yellow brick road, and following it despite obstacles or tempting detours is ultimately what you seek. It is a way for those who desire to live a Connected Life to know they are part of a much larger vibration. I say *vibration* because it moves us beyond conversations of spiritual faith and changes the concept of life and the world by putting it in energetic terms.

As an HR practitioner, your work landscape is less of the physical world and more so about the energetic one. Through culture, potential hires, and employee relations, you are navigating the energetic body of the organization. Choosing to live and work, in alignment with your golden brick road of connection, magnifies your capacity to do this work by honoring yourself and others you encounter. When we travel this path, we acknowledge and fully accept that every encounter is intentional. When we travel this path, we open ourselves to seeing that which goes unnoticed or unseen, embracing a constant evolving transparency of understanding. It is this path that makes our work as practitioners game changing, world healing, and an absolute organizational necessity.

A Foundational Formula

While how to live in alignment with your path will materialize in a collection of daily practices unique to you, there is a foundational formula that can aid in initial guidance. This formula is the approach for how we care for the energetic body in Medical Qigong with the true intent of eventually helping the patient establish a conscious inner harmony. Conscious inner harmony is a physical, mental, and spiritual state of peace that the individual is fully aware of. Living in alignment with your Connected Path means obtaining conscious inner harmony. It is through alignment that you experience a vibration so internally peaceful that you know without a doubt it is serving your highest good and purpose.

The foundational formula includes three elements. In Medical Qigong, they are called *purging, tonification,* and *regulation.* For our purposes, we will utilize the terms of *clear, cultivate,* and *connect.* A version of these elements is embedded in this book. Right now you have done some serious clearing mixed with a bit of cultivation, and in a moment you will learn how to engage in a personal practice to cultivate even more.

Let's take a look at the formula's elements individually to fully understand each objective.

Clear

The primary objective of clearing is to remove from the energetic body all that does not serve our greatest good. This includes emotions, thought patterns, and belief systems. This portion of the formula does not aim at forgetting or erasing memories or past experiences, but rather to sort through and claim the wisdom while releasing the fear. There is always a fear component that accompanies growth. When not released as a seedling, it sprouts roots in our mind, embedding pathways that cause fear-based reactions we experience today in a matter of seconds.

Cultivate

I wish it was instilled in all of us as children that our energy is precious. Instead we live daily, depleting it as if it is a boundless source, and as a result we end our days exhausted. During one of my recent social media scrolls, I came across a post on Instagram by @bespiritual_ with 4,624 likes titled: *9 Warning Signs You're Mentally and Emotionally Exhausted*:

1. Easily Irritated
2. Completely Unmotivated

3. Anxiety or Panic Attacks

4. Trouble Sleeping

5. No Patience

6. Indigestion

7. Crying Unexpectedly

8. Detached from Reality

9. You Feel Empty

These are all symptoms that occur when our energy is depleted. The primary objective of cultivation is to replenish our energetic reserves, increase our energy levels, and invite restorative energy from external pure sources like the earth and sun. To be a healer requires dipping into energetic reserves. Therefore, these reserves need to be filled in order to support the work we are doing and boost our overall resiliency.

Connect

Through clearing and cultivating, your energetic body will be transformed into a vessel that can deliver and be of service to your highest potential. But to sustain this vessel, it is necessary to maintain a connection. This connection ensures that you stay attuned with the vibrations of your soul in order to live in alignment with your Connected Path. The primary objective of connection is to experience moments of inner peace that provide clarity and affirmation for your work.

Design a Practice

Now that you know the primary objective of the three elements of the foundational formula, it is time to begin building your own personal practice. The first design will serve you where you are today. It should provide a safe space for you to engage while still expanding your edges. Your personal practice will be a continuous evolution, always half a step ahead of your growth rate. Therefore, pay special attention to cues of comfort, when you find yourself mindlessly going through the act—it is a signal that it is time to adapt and advance your practice.

Designing your practice is fairly simple. It merely requires choosing an act of clearing, cultivating, and connecting. One act from each element is perfectly acceptable for an initial practice, engaging in as few acts from each element is acceptable, too. You might also find yourself being intuitively guided to do one act of clearing, multiple acts of cultivating throughout the day, and a few acts of connecting before bedtime. All of these materializations of the foundational formula are acceptable versions of a personal practice.

I do have three recommendations to maximize the potential benefits of your practice:

1. The practice must serve you. This means you should feel as though the practice you designed is meeting you where you are today. If the acts are too challenging or even too easy, the likelihood increases that you will "check out" and not meet the intended objective. This also means you might have to be flexible. If you are super tired and one of your common acts of connection is a 30-minute seated meditation, you might have to instead complete a 5-minute meditation lying down. Both acts will achieve the primary objective of connecting, so don't become so rigid in your formula that you force acts, making them counterproductive.

2. The practice must contain an act from each element. If you choose to simply focus on one element, you run the risk of creating imbalance in your energetic body. This has the potential to trigger erratic emotional outbursts, excessive energy levels that feel like they cannot be contained, or overall disconnection.

3. The frequency of the practice is important, but consistency is critical. Ideally, you should practice every day. Yet it is better to practice twice a week, every week, than one Monday periodically per month for a year. Choose a starting

place that you can commit to for consistency, knowing that commitment is set in stone. Frequency may change from time to time, but the consistency of showing up for your practice cannot.

Let's now explore what acts could possibly serve each element in the formula.

Acts that Clear

Actions that can be utilized as part of your personal practice for clearing are not limited to the visualization and breathing exercises we have already utilized. However, if those served you greatly, they can certainly be used as a *clearing act* for your initial personal practice design.

Clearing acts are any act that allows you to release what does not serve you. This could include journaling, artistic expressions of music, kickboxing, running, recreational destruction, or even therapy and counseling. You simply need to ensure that your intention behind the action is releasing.

Recreational destruction, the trend of rage rooms and break rooms, provides a service where individuals can reserve a room simply to destroy things. The concept I think could be fun under pretty much any circumstance, however if this is intended to be a clearing act, I suggest entering the space with the intention of releasing whatever does not serve you. Then with each item you destroy, you are actually releasing.

For most of us, when you find your clearing act, it will feel good. Typically upon completion it leaves you feeling lighter. Therefore, if you're a runner like my husband, this about how you feel at the completion of your run. The same goes for artists and musicians—does engaging in the act leave you feeling like you were able to let something go? If instead, you feel like the act filled you up, then it is not a clearing act... it is actually an act of cultivating.

Acts that Cultivate

When you engage in acts of cultivation they will leave you feeling filled up. Therefore, many of the acts listed for clearing could possibly be an act of cultivation for you instead. For me I have found that creativity is a massive act of cultivation—everything from brainstorming, singing, creating connected canvases, and writing. As an active student of Medical Qigong, I kept insisting that my cultivation practice needed to consist of traditional Qi cultivation exercises. Yet I discovered that writing daily for 30-minutes filled me up even more than 30-minutes of traditional Qigong exercises.

Another act that cultivates that is severely misjudged is rest. Sleep is absolutely an act of cultivation. Choosing to honor your body's natural clock, by going to bed early or providing permission for a solid eight hours of rest, counts. Choosing to pause midday and partake in a 20-minute nap counts. The catch to acts of cultivation is these acts will not leave you feeling drained. Therefore, if you force yourself to get on the Peloton bike only to finish the workout to feel even more exhausted than when you started, you were not cultivating. In fact, you were actually using up your reserves that you ultimately are trying to replenish.

Acts that Connect

Acts that provide connection allow you to connect and experience a peaceful vibration. These acts produce beautiful moments that are only needed for a few minutes to meet the intention. The first act of connection that I could recognize happened during my first yoga class. At the conclusion of a yoga flow, traditionally the final asana is *Shavasana,* otherwise known as "corpse pose." Shavasana consists of laying flat on your back, while the yoga instructor leads you through visualization cues to completely relax. It was when I finally permitted myself to embrace the stillness that I had an act of connection. What I experienced during this pose was my version of a meditative state. Yoga provided me the weekly space to fine tune this act. I now engage in a version of this pose right before bed strictly for the purpose of connection.

After becoming aware of what an act of connection truly felt like when experienced, I was able to identify three other acts of connection we frequently engage in. The first is church. If you are an individual of faith who has found a spiritual home, I can almost guarantee you experience an act of connection when there. Secondly, if you love music or movies and have immersed yourself in fully experiencing either, you have experienced an act of connection. Finally is the act of taking a deep breath. The subtle soothing vibration you feel on the exhale is an act of connection.

Strength Training for the Healer

To prepare you for what's to come, this personal practice will be an absolute necessity. Take some time today and design your initial practice to begin tomorrow. Each day that you clear, cultivate, and connect will make you stronger and take you one step closer to what's possible.

CHAPTER NINE

ARTICULATING WHAT'S POSSIBLE

"We are all gifted with the magical ability of imagination, and when we open up to it, we become a conduit for a divine vision greater than our own." —Colette Baron Reid

I have spent most of my life feeling like I got shortchanged on the answers of life. From a young age, I believed I knew instinctively that every experience and encounter that life had to offer was a lesson. In the metaphysical text, *A Course in Miracles,* they describe the course of life as such:

> "Teaching is a constant process; it goes on every moment of the day, and continues into sleeping thought as well."

Yet with every year, I felt like life was lacking on delivery of the lessons. I mean, I learned something but not the *something* I was really needing or wanting. It wasn't until my final year of graduate school that the first veil of transparency on work would be lifted. It was during my master's degree capstone course that Dr. Jo Tyler shared a participant inquiry research theory by John Heron and Peter Reason called *Four Ways of Knowing.*

At first when I saw this theory, depicted in a triangle visual aid graphic that echoed commonalities of how Maslow's hierarchy of needs is often portrayed, I was unimpressed. The four ways of knowing consisted of the following:

- Experiential: knowing directly through experience
- Presentational: knowing through artful means

- Propositional: knowing conceptually
- Practical: knowing through skillful doing

The triangle portrayed experiential at the base, with presentational above, then propositional and finally practical at the tippy top. It seemed pretty basic to me. Of course we learn when we experience something, and then understand it conceptually, and eventually apply it to our lives. However, Dr. Tyler's emphasis was on our lack of engaging in presentational knowing. She argued that not exploring our experiential knowledge through a presentational or "artful" lens allowed lessons to remain unacknowledged or misinterpreted. This causes flawed or incomplete conceptual conclusions that then become the basis for life application and growth.

After this lecture, I couldn't help but express sarcastically to Dr. Tyler that I thought this theory was phooey (being a technical term) and would therefore make this course a waste of time. This was after she had disclosed that this theory would be the basis of our coursework, and how we would spend the semester exploring our true lessons and outcomes from the program using artful expression. I remember reiterating to her that I thought it was ridiculous to waste a whole semester on art projects when I needed to have knowledge I could tangibly translate into action. This was the master's program my employer required me to acquire while assisting with the tuition.

This was the exact moment that Dr. Tyler became one of the greatest teachers of my life. She remained cool, calm, and collected with a smile on her face. "Humor me," she said. "Be open this semester and if at the end, it generates useless outcomes I will consider removing it from the curriculum for future capstones." If you haven't been able to tell yet, I was a passionate young professional with a heavily ego-driven mouth. I was too big for my britches.

What happened next? I had a life-changing semester. That semester was the birth of my work today and the concluding comment from Dr. Tyler after watching me that semester. "You can't stay in corporate. Your work is not meant to be contained." She saw something in me then, a path for myself that was bigger than I could ever envision. But unfortunately, that is what growing up does to us. It doesn't stop our ability to imagine, it simply casts judgment, instantaneously convincing us those things can't ever be possible, so why bother. This leaves us believing that mediocrity is the measurement for professional aspiration and hopes of changing the world are left for superheroes, in other words categorized as fantasy.

The Gift of 2020

In March 2020, a wave of stillness was experienced as individuals experienced a massive shutdown as a result of COVID-19. Life for the first time came with a pause button. Along with this stillness came an invitation to turn inward, an invitation that often goes unnoticed due to the rapid chaotic pace we commonly navigate.

Recently, while reconnecting with a friend, I asked how he was doing and he raised his arm, presenting it horizontally about chest high and said. "If this is the waterline then my nose is peeking just above the surface, just enough for life sustaining air. That is how I am." What a powerful image that describes the pressure and exhaustiveness of most of our workloads, despite living in a literal oxymoron during quarantine, working from home. This transition of physical workspace deceived us into thinking that more balance had been obtained between these two worlds, yet the shift only blurred the unhealthy boundaries many were already abiding. Safe to say we are back to a status quo where the invitation to turn inward is once again able to be easily ignored.

This might come as a relief to you, especially since the invitation is always accompanied by its close friend and confidant, discomfort. It's sad and surreal to realize we lack an intimate knowing or connection with ourselves. It is the one relationship we've all taken for granted, believing there could be no possible way to lose it. Yet it was amidst the stillness of 2020 that a multitude of people recognized they had lost themselves.

Despite the frustration that followed this new awareness and awakening, this act of recognition itself was the great gift of 2020. In my work, I saw clients come out of the quarantine with little resistance to reflect at depths not usually tapped during typical Leadership Development work. I found myself met with fewer walls and more so navigating the aftermath of the processing the rubble from the fall. Most importantly, I was met with a desire from more individuals who embraced the inward invitation.

Inward Conversations Through Images

It is important to accept that when it comes to mastering conversation with self, it is literally an art. The primary challenge that often derails people from continuing this personal development is that it does not materialize in a "normal" fashion when it comes to talking to ourselves.

When we imagine talking to ourselves, we often think of times when we have had literal inner dialogue. Makes sense, since this is the literal act and definition of what we are seeking. However, the conversations and knowledge you are seeking do not have the capacity for common linguistics. Language, as we have come to know and experience it, is communication at a surface level. Even that dialogue in our mind that we just referenced is surface. Yet your desire now is to go beyond the surface. If I were to build on my friend's waterline example, I would say that to find what you are seeking, it requires leaving the safety of the surface and diving into the dark depths of the water below.

If you were actually going to begin diving in to the water, you wouldn't plan on an immersion that would leave you without access to air. It is essential to return to the surface periodically for air. It is what brings materialization to all we discover in the depths.

The easiest way I have found to teach others the language of our selves is using a method of creating a Connected Canvas. This method produces a visual outcome of images that collectively come together to share a message from self. It is through the abstract nature of image collection that we can release our need for logic and allow ourselves to simply listen. As the expression goes, a picture is worth a thousand words. Each image possesses the potential to share a multitude of messages, bringing a breadth that can only be described as magical.

For years I have brought individuals together in a community fashion to create Connected Canvases in January during an event called Vision Fest. My intention has always been to combat the trend of traditional Vision Boards, that are driven by the need to logically articulate our goals. Instead, I wanted to provide a process that provides the opportunity to listen and acknowledge that perhaps surface level logic does not know what is best for our highest good. Each year, I find it fascinating to find the individuals who come open to embrace the process of listening and those who struggle to understand what could be possible if they were to release an ounce of forced control while creating.

The clear cue that signals a Connected Canvas was done correctly is found in its ability to whisper. The maker of the canvas is never able to clearly articulate its meaning, but they always know that each image moves them in a powerful way. The messages that are shared on these canvases can be fully revealed if you provide yourself the space and openness to listen. Yet I have found that for most this reflection is still too overwhelming, uncomfortable, and therefore rarely experienced.

In my private coaching practice, I use this method to assist clients when they are struggling with questions that can only be answered by going within. In these circumstances, the clients are often so frustrated with their current situation that they are only able to complete this process with the assistance of a guide who chunks the method into digestible amounts. Most of the time they are completely unaware of the desired outcome and are also desperate to find some sort of clarity on how to move forward.

I share these observations so that you may provide yourself with reasonable expectations as you embark on using this method for perhaps the first time. There will be a direct consequence if you apply any unnecessary pressure to yourself or this process, where you will likely find yourself frustrated and unable to complete the task at hand. Instead, focus on the objective and true intention here. This method will provide you a platform to engage in a conversation with your soul, while inviting the expression of what's truly possible to be revealed. Let go of context and requirements, while embracing trust that your highest self will serve your highest good in this moment.

Create Your Connected Linguistic Library

The Merriam Webster dictionary defines linguistics as:

the study of human speech
including units, nature, structure,
and modification of language.

It is time for you to begin to study the language of your inner voice, to discover the many facets it utilizes to get your attention and attempt to communicate. When I first began my intuitive development, I was working with a holistic life coach who explained this language as a spiritual library. She shared that our intuitive senses may have common broad definitions, yet how they materialize for each of us is different and unique.

There are many reasons for this, but the primary one is that we each need the language that would be most effective in conversation with us. That ideal language reflects our intricate individuality in hope of minimizing our resistance of receipt. This spiritual library comes alive almost like a legend, a personalized map explaining the symbols used for communication. This exercise will utilize a Connected Canvas to do exactly that—provide a map of the symbols your inner voice uses for communication.

As in previous exercises, this one begins with intention. Along with that, you will need a collection of magazines. (This is my preferred method—call me *old school*.) However, if you do not have access or self-select to opt out of locating magazines, you can use the internet. My personal recommendation is to use the website Unsplash.com. I will provide direction for both methods.

1. Set an intention. Say the bold-faced sentence below silently in the mind or out loud. Remember, even if it feels silly, if this is what you desire then the intention will indeed be set.

   Higher Self, show me our language.

2. Spend small increments of time, no longer than 15-20 minutes, paging through magazines or scrolling through Unsplash.com. Rip out or save any image that resonates with you. The reason for resonation does not need to be clear. The key is to tune into subtle vibrations within. When a shift occurs, do not question it. Simply capture the image that triggered it. If using magazines, attempt to gravitate toward images over words. Text should only be collected if it is screaming at you to collect it, meaning you'll know when you should include it.

3. These small increments of time should span over several days and perhaps even months. In between, store your images in a desktop folder or manila envelope where you can easily locate them. Resist the temptation to revisit the images collected during this time. Simply continue to add images.

4. Once you feel your collection period is complete, it is now time to revisit the images. Review each one and remove any images that resonate significantly less than the others. Avoid using reason and ignore any rationale that attempts to creep in telling you that an image makes no sense and should be discarded. If it resonates and speaks with you strongly, it stays. Magazine collectors can trim down the images during this step, isolating and highlighting what you selected. After you have reviewed your images, determine if you still have enough to continue. This is a personal decision. You will simply know if it feels right to continue. If not, return to steps 2 and 3 until you complete step 4 again and are ready to continue.

5. For this step, magazine collectors will need a canvas, poster board, or paper. The size is completely up to you. My digital creators will need PowerPoint, Keynote or Google Slides. Begin to organize your images on your canvas. Digital creators may choose to create one slide or a slide show. Play and arrange until you feel every image has found its place. Some images will not make the cut and that is okay. This is an intuitive-driven process. It is critical to trust and not question yourself. The canvas is complete when you feel it is so.

Reading the Canvas

Your canvas can materialize in a multitude of ways, even some I have not even experienced or witnessed. The best advice is to recognize that any reaction produced by the board and images is intentional. Therefore, if you are looking at an image of a man and it reminds you of a time when you were sad, perhaps emotions are a method of communication from your inner voice. Or perhaps it is the specific memory that came to mind that reveals a moment when your Higher Self was attempting to reach you and you need to reflect on what possibly you missed. Or perhaps it's the individual who made you sad, what they said or did. Was the message literally shared with you by a person and act occurring at a specific moment by design?

Finally, don't pressure yourself to be able to read your board immediately following creation. In fact, don't put pressure on yourself to be able to read your board completely at all. From my experience, the board slowly reveals its answers at a pace where we can optimally absorb what is being shared. Therefore, instead place the board in a location where you will encounter it often and allow it to whisper as needed.

CHAPTER TEN

THE ART OF INTERNAL CHECK-INS

"The decision to make the present moment into your friend is the end of ego." —Eckhart Tolle

One of the most frequently asked questions I encounter is, "What is ego?" I often reference the concept of ego when describing what is happening to an individual who is living out of alignment from their Connected Path. In simplistic terms, the ego is your survival wisdom shared from your reptilian brain. It is ego that makes us human. According to MacLean's Triune Brain Model, the reptilian or primal brain, "controls our innate and automatic self-preserving behavior patterns, to ensure our survival and that of our species." These innate self-preserving behavior patterns are often referred to as the four Fs: Feeding, Fighting, Fleeing, and an F-Word that by definition means reproduction.[11]

The dominant source of fuel for the ego is fear. Fear is the ego's most powerful form of influence. It is the root emotion that causes us to routinely question and hesitate. Whether it is fear of failure, not being accepted, or worthy, this doubt is driven by the ego's desire to maintain control.

Now before you instantly begin viewing your ego as a villain, I want you to know that the ego's intentions are good. The ego wants to protect you. It truly only wants to keep you safe. Therefore it's not so much about silencing the ego indefinitely, but more about

---

[11] https://www.interaction-design.org/literature/article/our-three-brains-the-reptilian-brain

bringing balance to the ego's presence so it does not limit your potential.

I know this completely contradicts the Eckhart Tolle quote that hints at an ultimate desire to end the ego. But here's the thing. As you find yourself functioning more dominantly in a space where you are Connected, you will find yourself depending less and less on the ego. Being Connected serves you in a way that the ego cannot, while also being able to replace the ego in nearly all facets.

As you strengthen yourself as a Connected being, you will become attuned in a way that could not compare to any self-preserving behaviors designed to strictly protect your physical human form. Being Connected speaks to a recognition that we are part of something much bigger than ourselves. This is the truth you've already discovered if you found yourself openly embracing the idea that you are a healer as an HR Practitioner. You know you play a role in ending suffering that was initially created by workplaces, workplaces that are the byproduct of visionaries with foresight driven by ego, making these workplaces not evil, but simply a creation of someone's hope for survival with systems and structures materialized from a place of fear. It is these environments that will need your healing gift most, and in the next section of this book, we will begin discussing how to begin that healing work.

However, now knowing that the work you are being called to do will require not only quieting your own ego but will also aiding others in quieting theirs, the question becomes less about "What is ego?" and more about "What do I do about my ego?"

Ego-ic Releases

In Chapter 8, we designed your personal practice that consisted of clearing, cultivating, and connecting. I hope you have begun your practice, working toward a daily habit of clearing, cultivating, and connecting in some facet, even if for only a few minutes.

Ego-ic Releases are a form of internal check-ins. These will become a resource to you as you continue strengthening your capacity in functioning from a Connected space. These internal check-ins are about giving yourself grace, recognizing that we are indeed human and that the ego periodically chimes in or takes over. Personally, I still find myself succumbing to ego during intuitive coaching sessions or while treating energetically. Whispers of...

What are you doing?

This doesn't work.

Who are you to do this work?

At first, I would find myself instantly distracted by ego, ending up in an internal argument between fear and faith. Now I find the answer is not in resolving but rather in releasing what ego presents. The act is similar to the exercise of quieting the monkey mind, when we allow thoughts to present themselves, be recognized, and pass through without judgment. These internal check-ins are about doing the same when ego presents itself.

The Forms of Ego

My journey of being Connected to disconnected and then finding my way back, showed me the greatest form of ego. When we spend time refusing to be ourselves, terrified of rejection that accompanies the vulnerability of showing your pure self to the world, we can only live with one other alternative. We spend our days as someone else, specifically we spend our days being what others want us to be, or we spend our days being what others believe us to be. As this way of life grows and evolves, it becomes our roles of identity and more complex self-preserving behaviors.

It is this evolution that explains how a massive introvert like me can come to be an expected extrovert, living for decades, draining myself in social settings that served nothing but my ego. Ego begins as sabotaging inner dialogue but when it is permitted to fester, it becomes forms of identity. It becomes the response to the question of I am.

I am angry.

I am a mother.

I am not worthy.

Each "I am" statement only further generates expectations that lead to greater disconnection from ourselves. This leads us to ask only one logical question: "How do we stop this disconnection from ourselves? Can we actually achieve such a task if it is truly this embedded in our way of life?" The answer is yes and it is possible to stop this disconnection from occurring. The answer comes in mastering the habit of ego-ic releases, so it is a natural response to ego. It is only when this habit becomes second nature that you will potentially discover it is no longer needed.

Why a Habit Is Needed

Think back to my example of ego chiming in during my client sessions. Did this bring to mind any instances for you? Ego tends to show up at moments when we are weakest—experiencing triggering life events filled with heightened emotions of sadness, anger, fear, anxiety, or doubt. We are weakest when our immune systems are compromised and when we are tired or exhausted. Ego seeks prime opportunities of least resistance when we have a lack of energy to push back or a desire to dwell in the emotion. These moments unfortunately make up a large chunk of our professional lives.

As HR Practitioners, the price of making ourselves available to serve others comes with an increased exposure. Not only do you have to navigate moments you personally encounter, you also can be exposed to moments encountered by others who might seek you out for release. In working with HR practitioners as well as facilitating my own personal healing, I have discovered a vast part of the damage is a result of what I have taken on from others. In most cases, I know I absorbed their heightened emotions in hopes to help, never knowing the actual toll it was taking on my body.

In order to combat the frequency of these opportunities for ego, we must utilize a counteractive process that instills opportunities for connection at the same rate. That is what ego-ic releases create—moments for connection. These moments can occur in a matter of minutes or you can choose to partake in moments that last for an hour of more. These moments are invitations to check in with yourself and can manifest in a multitude of ways, however I want to share with you the ones I have found personally serve me the most during this time of growth.

To do this, I am going to share with you three levels of check-ins. We will begin with the more "complex" and then end with the more simplistic check-ins.

Naps

In *The HR Intuitive*, I shared a story about my initial struggle to grasp the concept of napping during the day as a normal practice. Yet here I am now with a nap chair in my office and a common practice of a 22-minute nap around noon. The duration wasn't planned, but 22-minutes was the time determined by my body once I gave it permission to engage in this ritual of rest. Every time I engage in this ritual, I am naturally awakened at the 22-minute mark.

Rest is pretty much the gold standard when it comes to an act of restoration. However, as I began to fully embrace this 22-minute midday rest ritual, I started to notice sudden powerful differences in the nature of my sleep between night and day. My midday rest was accompanied with a subtle vibration that almost instantly invited me into this beautiful state between conscious and unconsciousness. It is this vibration that I have come to associate with being Connected. Many times my rest rituals begin in this state and I gradually drift into a state of nothingness, where I then return at the conclusion of 22-minutes.

To further reiterate the depths of these check-ins, I want to semi-digress by exploring the meaning behind the numerical duration that was revealed during my practice. The number 22 is said to appear as confirmation of the power of your inner divinity.

Nature

Since I've opened myself to embracing the concept of energy, I have found that nature is one of its most purest and powerful sources. This is probably not a huge surprise. If we simply consider air and water as examples, they are absolute necessities for life—they give us life. So when we seek out additional opportunities to connect to this powerful source, we welcome a beautiful reminder of all that we seek.

In the second episode of the show *Down to Earth* on Netflix, Darin Olien introduces Zac Ephron to the concept of grounding. It is after they travel to France via the Channel Tunnel, that Darin suggests they pull over to ground themselves to the new country. He invites Zac to remove his shoes and come feel the earth, an idea that Zac is convinced initially is a joke. Regardless, they both find themselves out by the side of the road feeling the blades of grass and breathing in the fresh air. At the end, Zac admits to it feeling good yet still hints at skepticism to the grounding concept.

For a nature check-in, I am not even going to suggest to partake in grounding unless you feel moved to. I am strictly going to encourage you to get outside and to take it one step further, get outside in nature. Whether that is a trip to a local park, going for a hike, or strolling in the sand oceanside, there is a powerful undeniable force when you place yourself in its presence. When I embark on one of these nature check-ins, I almost immediately feel a tingling warmth on my palms upon simply setting the intention.

No, I don't want to.

This Connected Check-in was the first one I mastered. I've literally been practicing it since I was a girl. It's a bit unconventional, however, if nature is the purest source of energy and naps are the gold standard of restoration, this is the strongest Connected Check-in.

Now, to understand this practice there are two fundamental truths that you must recognize at some level. The first is that the common spiritual act of prayer is less about filing a request and more about conversation. When we engage in prayer with the sole intent of asking for what we need, we provide space for our ego to flourish. This is the literal equivalent of telling your ego that it knows best. It knows better than, depending on your belief system, Source, the Divine, or the Universe. This small act removes you from the concept that you are part of something bigger and emphasizes sole accomplishment with blatant disregard for their ripple effect.

The second is that you have free will. When I first learned about the concept of soothsayers, I thought instantly that they had all the answers. If they knew my fate, destiny, and future, they could save me a lot of anguish by providing me the roadmap rather than me having to engage in so much self-exploration. In actuality, fortune tellers only share the path as it appears in the present moment. This path has the capacity to shift at any given time, because you are empowered to change your mind at any given time. The concept of being able to predict the future, is built on the basis that future outcomes are predictable based on a set of given circumstances. However, this should never be confused with the fact that you indeed always have a choice. You can change your mind and literally your life at any time.

The "No, I don't want to" check-in practice is a combination of inner debate and prayer. When we commonly debate whether we want to do something or not, that counterparty is still ourselves. In this check-in practice the counterparty is our Connected selves or path. The difference is experienced in the topic of the debate. The dilemma in question will be regarding something you *know* you should do yet are resisting because of fear. No matter how clearly Connected it is, this does not dismiss the trust needed to continue. Our Connected Paths are filled with growth points that we might intuitively recognize as necessary, but instinctively identify as terrifying. It is this beautiful dance that gave birth to the "No, I don't want to" check-in.

In this practice, you are actually having a conversation with Spirit. It is this practice that I use when I engage in the act of prayer. I believe it encourages the cultivation of a deep, intimate relationship with Self and Spirit. In its organic form, our arguments for why we don't want to do what's next are created by the ego and in this check-in we get the opportunity to experience a level of Divine intervention.

Music

Music has been the one check-in that has sustained me through it all. Despite all my useless attempts at resisting, music was the one method of connection that persisted. The reason for its resilience is that music's presence is almost impossible to avoid. It's played in the background at stores, restaurants, and elevators. It has become an essential tool for covering up uncomfortable silence.

This check-in happens unprompted and unsolicited, materializing as a song or tune that speaks to you. Whether it is the actual lyrics speaking to you word by word or the thoughts and feelings that arise within you while listening, they are all a part of this Connected Check-in.

If you are curious as to why and how music can be so powerful organically, the answer is pretty straightforward. Music is a tangible manifestation of connectedness. Its muse is Spirit.

Make

Now that I have shared with you that it is the creation process that makes music such a powerful resource, it should only make logical sense that then any sort of creation process would result in a Connected Check-in. I was tempted to initially share this check-in from strictly an artistic lens, yet that would not be an accurate depiction of all the manners in which this check-in could materialize.

The key element that identifies whether a creation process would classify or cause a check-in comes in the capacity of being able to get lost in the present. Therefore, regardless of whether the creation process is building a birdhouse, planting a garden, refinishing furniture, or painting an abstract, if you find yourself getting lost in the moment, you are partaking in a Connected Check-in. It is in our ability to fully embrace the now, where we naturally can release our concerns for the future and the past, that we create a space where ego is unable to take form and we are one with the formless.

Move

For me the most effective Connected Check-in that is caused by movement comes as spontaneous dance parties. A true tradition in the Smeltzer household, it is a common and expectant accordance that I fully believe is the sole reason we have Alexa devices throughout the house. No matter where we are we can say, "Alexa, play me a dance song," and she delivers.

After studying Chinese Medicine for the past few years, I now have a better understanding why this act is so effective at making us feel good, courtesy of dopamine, but also so much clearer. It is because of the fact that we are indeed a clearer vessel at the conclusion of our spontaneous dance party that creates a perfect environment for connection to occur.

When we engage in movement, especially those of the nature of quick erratic dance routines, we often are literally shaking the body. This shaking motion allows us to release energetic stagnations that do not serve us. Think about it this way. Have you ever picked up something yucky that wouldn't come off of your hand so you engage in a violent vigorous shaking motion in hopes of it detaching? Same concept with energy that you accumulate during the day that makes you feel yuck... and trust me we accumulate a lot of it.

Therefore, what I am talking about in regards to a Connected Check-in, driven by my movement, will incorporate motion that allows the body to physically release us from the ego.

Offline

Technology has evolved to a perceived necessity in our society. Its convenience and accolades for efficiency have created a lifestyle overflowing with things to do. We treat our lives like a suitcase being packed for vacation. Technology brings these new products designed to maximize the space in our luggage to pack even more. As a result, my suitcase that used to hold maybe two pairs of shoes, five outfits and my makeup, now holds six pairs of shoes, twenty outfits, a pile of beauty products, and a few books if I sit on it while I zip it up.

Our to do lists are the ego's distraction list. The more occupied we are, the less likely we are to challenge our ego. The more we have to do leaves us with even less time to recover, so to be frank, you're too tired to challenge ego.

But since this is our norm, the act of simply going offline for a period of minutes can allow a Connected Check-In to occur. Try walking away from technology fully for a few minutes. Trust me, it will be okay. The world will not end. In fact, you'll find that it will all be there waiting for you upon your return.

Oasis

I believe it is innately built into our bodies to seek out a happy place. For some this happy place is a beach, a lake, the forest, a museum, or even an outlet mall. We routinely feel a nudge to return to these places because vibrationally they deliver a nourishing energy.

For me, my happy place is Disneyland, which sounds cliche since it was designed to be the happiest place on earth. But when I walk through those entrance gates, it never fails to shift my energy. I could spend the whole day sitting on park benches and taking it in. Not only do I recognize this, but see it as well—there's just something about me in Disneyland.

These happy places are special pockets of Connectedness. When you feel rundown and beaten by ego, go to them.

Oxygen

Breath is a practice that will continue to be encouraged. This basic act, that we must do to live, also has the potential to connect us deep within. This Connected Check-in is only enhanced when combined with intention. It has the ability to quiet the ego's loud rants and recenter us, so we are able to move forward confidently within minutes.

There's a universal understanding of the power breath has, that's why it is so common to hear, *Take a deep breath*, anytime you are experiencing heightened emotions. The coaching comments come from loved ones and sometimes even supportive strangers as an instinctual response to help you in the moment. This means the practice is one of divine intervention. When we need it the most, we will be led to engage in a breath practice, even by means of physical intervention.

I'll leave you with one final thought regarding breath. In the book *A New Earth* by Eckhart Tolle, he is asked by an individual for advice regarding their continued development through formal courses. Tolle responds, "Be aware of your breathing as often as you are able, whenever you remember. Do that for one year, and it will be more powerfully transformative than attending all of these courses. And it's free."

No Minimum Obligation

These nine Connected Check-ins share my evolution of practice. Playfully, I intentionally titled terms to be presented in alphabetical order of NMO. If we think about the journey to restore ourselves back to pure self as the alphabet, "Z" would stand for *zombie*, equating to the massive dissonance within. The dictionary defines a zombie as a person who is lifeless and completely unresponsive to their surroundings. "A" would stand for *awakened,* equating to the state of consciousness possessed within. Keeping this scale in mind, the "N" check-ins of *naps, nature,* and *no conversations*, are more evolved than the "O" check-ins of *offline, oasis,* and *oxygen*.

I intentionally selected terms associated with letters toward the center of the alphabet because I am still actively on my journey and do not believe that I'm letters away from "A." I still have a great deal of healing to do within, and I hope this provides hope and inspiration regarding your own journey. It might seem daunting as you begin to truly see what this path entails, but know that every intentional step in the right direction is literally a milestone within itself.

If we transform my playful NMO alphabet analogy into an acronym, it would stand for "No Minimum Obligation." Moving forward especially in regard to these check-ins, there is no minimum requirement. This growth and restorative evolution is yours alone and therefore the pace should be dictated strictly by you. As someone who has desired to force and rush my own healing, I have found my Connected Path routinely delivers detours and roadblocks. Yet these detours and roadblocks are not about ego distraction, but more so patience. The pace that is instilled within us associated with success is more rapid than we were ever meant to endure. It's no wonder so many are suffering from "work-life balance" dilemmas. In reality, we are simply suffering from a lack of balance overall—individually, collectively, and even environmentally.

Wherever you are today, do not allow ego to begin to use overwhelm as a tactic to derail you from starting. My only ask in this entire book is that you begin, wherever you feel called, no matter if it's a grand first move or a tiny shuffle forward. Do not allow your ego to instill self-doubt, doubt within yourself and the path. This is not an "As seen on TV" weight loss program, where I highlight my most successful stories. In fact, my previous books were written to establish the primer that I am just like everyone else.

Practice Makes Permanence

In a podcast interview with Jessica Brustad from the Playful Mind Project, she recommended a shift to a common phrase regarding practice. She said, "Practice doesn't make perfect; practice makes permanence." The act of engaging in these check-ins is not about perfection. I don't even believe such a thing as a perfect practice even exists and if it does that perfect practice would have to be entirely uniquely yours. There is no universal one serving practice for all, and therefore, there is no way anyone could judge your practice in reference to perfection.

What practice does is instill a habit. It creates consistency. Ultimately, isn't that what we are seeking? A consistent connection to ourselves and to our path? Begin these check-ins and create a practice to move toward permanence... permanence of connection, permanence of evolution, permanence of pure self.

PART THREE

THE HAWK
SHOWS US WHY
WE SHOULD CARE

CHAPTER ELEVEN

ORGANIZATIONAL ENERGIES

It's perfectly natural to feel overwhelmed after reading and doing the work of clearing and cultivating. Therefore, you may be entering this next phase with the belief that there is no way you can do the healing work that awaits. In fact, if you were like me when I was first exposed to these concepts, you hold the belief that it will take years of mastery to be able to do any of this.

Here is what I have learned. You can begin this work today and have an impact if you meet one classification. You must be an HR Practitioner who is doing this work because of the people. If you've been in the trenches of Human Resources for whatever duration because you care about people, you can do this work. It doesn't matter what your past experience is or what the path was that led you to the role. It is about what keeps you there.

Human Resources in its true artform is messy and exposes a lot of ugly, yet the beauty is found in the humanity we bring to the business. It is for this reason, that I constantly argue that the current definition is too restrictive and should expand to include all practitioners who seek to preserve humanity in business.

HR as Sensitive Beings

The reason why I devoted my work to HR professionals goes beyond me as the source of inspiration. My personal healing path required that I accept and embrace being sensitive. However, what I found as I accepted and shared this truth about me is that others began to step forward sharing similar experiences. Individuals were curious about my healing path because it resonated with them. Many of these individuals were my colleagues in the HR profession, whom I had assumed would have judged and abandoned me when they learned what I had been working on. In actuality, what was birthed was a new community of HR professionals, and my work was welcomed. For the first time I saw a vulnerability in the tough exterior armor many carry for survival.

As I have evolved as a practitioner and embraced my work as a healing modality, my sensitivities have heightened and become more succinct. As a result, when I now venture out to organizations to do an initial needs assessment, I can see the collective energies that are actively generating the organizational culture. Prior, I could sense energy but was unable to decipher the differences between the collective and how each individual's energy added or detracted. This shift allowed me to understand for the first time the energetic force HR practitioners encounter on a daily basis.

Without any experience on how to detect or decipher energy from its place of origin, HR practitioners are simply left to cope with the overwhelm of what we have come to call workplace drama and other people's baggage. In addition, this new revelation allowed me to see that the very thing that draws and keeps us devoted to this profession is also the greatest signal of sensitivity. Once I began training other HR practitioners on methods to protect and care for their energy, I noticed a stark difference between them and my other Qigong clients. These individuals were able to notice and sense the energy within them and around them much sooner. A skill that usually needs to be developed and is part of beginning Qigong training. That being said, I believe my HR tribe was destined to be the great caretakers of workplace energies and this skillset is innately embedded within.

As we begin this work, do not be surprised to discover that you are indeed sensitive and although what you detect may seem chaotic it will also be exhilarating. It will be freeing to be able to give a name to an aspect of your work that has been there all along. Know that as you continue clearing, cultivating, and practicing these techniques, your skill set will sharpen and your work will become more powerful. This is the cusp of organizational change and deep personal transformation. This is the arena I believe HR was destined to play in.

It Begins with Nothing

In the book *The Five-Element Solution* by Jean Haner, she describes the first step in an elemental sequence as beginning with water, translating it into the action of, doing nothing. If you read my book, *The HR Intuitive*, you know that water serves as my primary elemental constitution. Despite it being core to my natural make-up, I resisted to recognize this essential part of me for decades. The result was a very lost young adult wandering in a haze. The primal element that needed nourished within me to thrive was withering, and so was I. What is relevant here is the reason I refused to tend to this elemental nature. To care and nourish the water element requires us to let go of what we have been taught is necessary to be meaningful. This element requires a beautiful release of control, one accompanied with trust that what comes is as it is intended.

In our working world, it is ingrained that time is money, and to be successful you must be efficient and effective. In the world of working with people, this means we attempt to force resolutions. We enter environments expecting problems that we can solve and almost willing a solution to appear. Once we get a glimpse of a prospective issue we move directly to possible solutions, with little regard or respect to attempting to understand exactly what is being revealed. The result here is chaos and this is in fact what we are dealing with in many organizational cultures demanding change. By the time leadership seeks intervention it is complete and utter chaos. It is the compilation of layer upon layer of possible solutions to possible problems.

Those who are skilled in team and individual interventions experience marginal success in these circumstances because they typically can isolate a few definite problems. In times of chaos, there are obvious major concerns that rise to the surface that a practitioner can address. They are also more likely to have a better chance at comprehending these concerns, because the problems exist on a plane of expected business obstacles. The root cause that begins cultural decline is rare on this plane. Therefore, those concerns being addressed by the practitioners are symptoms of a suffering culture and treating them is only a bandage. Until the root cause is the focus of intervention, the symptoms will continue to return. It is this cycle that has birthed the common day for the HR Practitioners who spends their days putting out fires, an exhausting profession that many only manage for a few years before burning out and disengaging.

But how do we begin to identify a root cause that exists on a plane beyond our expectations? Even if we were fortunate enough to make contact with evidence for this root cause, how could we ever even recognize it as that? The answer is simple. We do not begin seeking when we believe there is a problem. Instead we begin today with the only intention to heighten our level of presence within the organization. We begin with the expectation of nothing, so that we may trust that what comes is what is intended. Therefore, even if as you read this, and knowing there is something rumbling beneath the surface of your organization, you need to be able to enter this reading expecting nothing. The expectation of nothing releases you of all pressure, and so there is no way for you to fail because there is nothing expected.

The Combination of Nothing and Sensitive

The combination of being a sensitive individual and mastering the expectation of nothing can lead to overwhelming insights. In contrast, an individual who lacks sensitivity and cannot find the state of nothingness will feel incessant frustration as they practice because of their inability to release control. It is natural for these individuals to subconsciously attempt to force the organizational reading into being, it is important to recognize if you are doing this because the outcomes from your readings will be tainted. In fact, what you will find is the readings produce outcomes for what you want to see like a mirror. These outcomes should be welcomed and used as further personal lessons almost like a guide showing you the personal path of development to nothingness.

If you are an individual experiencing overwhelming insights almost as though you were given new glasses to see your surroundings, take a deep breath and know that not every insight is a matter to be addressed. You are simply experiencing a new sense activating that will prove useful as you do your work. The insights you gain from a reading typically materialize in three ways:

1. The insight brings greater clarity to a circumstance you are already aware of.

2. The insight presents a possible outcome given the current trajectory.

3. The insight shines light on a new area that you need to pay attention to.

An Organizational Reading

I recognize that I quickly transitioned from organizational needs assessment to organizational reading. In my mind and for our purposes, they are one in the same and therefore these terms can be used interchangeably. You might find this helpful as you begin introducing or sharing this work with your organizational leaders or professional colleagues. I specifically decided to use the word *reading* because of its non-usage in the corporate environment. Its unfamiliarity works in our favor, attempting to assist in preventing you from defaulting to traditional assessment methodologies. The heavy focus and perceived requirement for objective assessments completely dismisses the subjectiveness that is human nature.

In an article by Bonnielee Cuevas, a meditation and yoga teacher, she describes intuitive readings as sessions facilitated by healers. She writes, "Healers are people that have a greater understanding of the energy around us and its powerful effect in our lives. The gift of healing is one that is studied on different levels and no healer will be the same. They will come from different backgrounds, education, and experiences that have led them to this incredible art, the gift of healing, the power of reading.[12]" You are a healer, your background, education, and experience is undoubtedly different than mine yet that does not discount your powerful ability.

An organizational reading is a needs assessment based on energy. It is the collective make-up of individual energies that create our organizational cultures, the living breathing personality of a company, or if you want to be more technical, its employment brand. Our culture is influenced by every individual that enters this collective body, bringing their unique energy to the space. Each new energy that enters or exits causes ripples that are felt through organizations big and small. Recruitment, when driven by gut feeling, is navigating the hiring process based on energy alignment. It is no surprise that energy is dynamic, and therefore it should not be surprising to recognize that so are our cultures. Therefore, we cannot sustain them at an ideal status quo. The human variable makes this impossible. Instead it is an art of caring for the culture, healing when necessary and cultivating always.

Let's revisit the three likely insights gained from an organizational reading now that you understand that you will be observing energy. It is important you accept this as a true artform. The materialization of these insights will vary based on your intuitive senses. All I can offer you is how these insights are revealed to me in hopes to open your mind and provide affirmation as you begin reading.

The insight brings greater clarity to a circumstance you are already aware of

My insights of this nature materialize as randomness, utter abstract thoughts when exploring a situation that I was already aware of. Take for example, you were conducting an employee investigation. While conducting the investigation, you felt compelled to ask a random question or perhaps it felt natural for you to check a

---

[12] https://medium.com/@bonnieleecuevas/what-is-an-intuitive-reading-4b12d21e7664

particular report or speak with another employee who was not obviously linked to the scenario. Regardless, the random act allowed you to see a dimension of the scenario that was not originally in your purview. For me personally, this materialized many times when dealing with sudden changes in employee performance.

The insight shines light on a new area that you need to pay attention to

For me, this insight began with what I will describe as an undeniable emotion or heightened awareness. It was like a part of me knew this was something I needed to pay attention to, that there was something there. During my years, when I was in the field immersed in Employee Relations, it was this insight that led me to dwell on particular on-site visits a little longer. Even though I would have no hard evidence or sometimes even a clue as to what could be occurring, I knew something was off. It was always like clockwork, after I departed the places after lingering, within days something would rise to the surface. Personally, I believe this is a result of a reaction to the ripple caused by my personal energy entering the collective energy of that location. This was especially true of worksites that had little contact with organizational senior leaders and therefore operating similar to an island, functioning however they wanted, creating their own little company culture. This is why, in the retail space, one store can feel so different based on location.

The insight presents a possible outcome given the current trajectory

For me, this insight materializes as a series of events observed in my mind's eye. The mind's eye is a phrase I simply use to describe the place in my head where I can observe a set of images while my eyes are open. These events typically play out the most likely outcome given the current emotional trajectory of all parties. I say *emotional* because, for the most part, it is how we feel in a moment that dictates our reactions. Therefore, that trajectory and the series of images you witness are subjective to constant change at any given moment an individual can change their mind. It's the beautiful gift of free will.

How To Conduct an Organizational Reading

To conduct an organizational reading requires three steps that can be easily remembered by the acronym of BIO. BIO stands for *Bubble, Interact, Observe.*

Step One. Bubble

This step must be completed before you enter the space where you hope to conduct the reading. It is necessary preparation that protects your energy as you reach out and interact with other energies present. It is best to complete this step in a space that is familiar and safe for you. You will need to be undisturbed for 10-15 minutes. During this time, you want to begin by focusing on your breath, allowing each deep inhale to take you inward. Take stock of your personal energy, with no judgment of whether it's good or bad, but more so creating a crystal-clear picture of what energy is yours.

Once you have become familiar with your current energetic presence, use your exhales to create a protective bubble around you. With every exhale, imagine you are expanding your protective energy away from your body, making the field more and more dense with each breathing sequence. You should feel a distinct disconnection and identifiable barrier between your personal energy and the external world. Once you can identify this barrier, step one is complete, and you may begin to conduct the reading.

Step Two. Interact

You are now ready to enter the space where you'd like to conduct the reading. For this step you will move around the space intentionally and intuitively. This means you should have an initial plan for how you will flow and interact through the space, however this plan should remain fluid, not a rigid framework. Your initial plan should be simple, nothing elaborate. For me, it is simply my intended route through the building and a list of all individuals I would like to have contact with. It is also best to ensure you have at least an hour to do the reading. You may complete it in less time; however, you never want to rush this process and you want to have the flexibility to dwell in places that call you.

As you enter the space and begin your walk-through, it best to think of your movement like water. You should flow through the space with a sense of wonder. Take your time to ensure that you can be fully present in each energetic element you encounter. This could be the energies of individual people, energy lingering in physical spaces, energies of external customers, as well as the collective energies as the interact. Your interactions throughout the space should serve in an effort to expose more energy.

Step Three. Observe

As you navigate the variety of energies, remain tuned to your senses with a heightened curiosity. Pay particular attention to shifts in emotions, random thoughts, and other sensations, knowing that they are all relevant. When we conduct an organizational reading, we enter the space with an intention to be of service, to be shown what we need to do the most beneficial work for the organization and the people who work there. It is this intention that makes all that is revealed relevant and purposeful.

Your primary focus while doing your walk-through is to pay close attention to what you are receiving. You should receive with open curiosity, where you take note for further exploration later. Do not become distracted by giving into doubts or analysis of what it all means. That will be for later. Readings are about receiving, remaining an open observing vessel.

Step Four. Log Observations

Once you have finished your walk-through and exited the space, immediately log all that you observed. Similar to how we began this process, there should be no judgment in what you are logging. There is no standard as to how these readings materialize. The observations are always unique to the practitioner conducting the reading. The observations also always only make sense to the practitioner conducting the reading. This reading is filled with messages for you to receive, no one else.

If you are concerned about forgetting things from the reading, feel free to carry a notebook to log notes throughout. However, you should not stop and fully log detailed observations. This act could potentially undo your preparation bubbling, ceasing the entire reading altogether. Therefore it is best to log simple words that will trigger your memory when you do your full log at the conclusion of the reading.

The purpose of this log is to capture all of your observations in a raw form. This is still not the time to begin analysis.

Step Five. Identify Insights

Now is the time to begin putting the puzzle together and seeing for the first time what your reading revealed. There are several ways to begin identifying your insights, but it is best to first attempt to discover which observations are connected. In other words, ask whether a potential collective insight or several smaller insights are connected.

Perhaps you identified the emotion of fear and anxiety existing in certain spaces or people. You realized upon closer look at your observation log that all these people work in the same space or report to the same supervisor. In addition to this theme, you have an innate knowing that the supervisor possibly is contributing in some way to the emotion being experienced.

Your raw observations are a series of connect-the-dots exercises, waiting to reveal a hidden image. Know that in some circumstances you won't yet have all the dots and therefore the revealed images are incomplete. If you practice tuning into yourself, you'll know when these circumstances occur, and you'll realize you are missing information.

You may also use the common organizational insights that I shared earlier in this chapter to assist you in beginning to identify your insights. However, do not lct those become your sole guide, limiting what you see. When it comes to intuitive work, the only true guide comes from within. Your readings will be spoken in words, seen in images, and felt in emotions that only you would fully understand. In other words, trusting yourself is non-negotiable.

Organizational Insights into Action

The manner in which these identified insights become tangible is up to you. The insights often provide a map regarding where you should begin your work, what work is most pressing, or what the purpose of your work should be.

When the insights reveal the place to start or what is most pressing, your action items are easy. You should begin there with the next logical step. Using our prior example of the possible supervisor contributing to fear and anxiety, I would probably find time to meet with that supervisor. This meeting would not be to confront them on what I found, but to continue the discovery process and see how their energy adds to the narrative. If your insights revealed an extremely unhappy employee, the next step would be to meet with them directly to check in. Inquire about how they are doing and share that you are concerned about them. The next steps after a reading are rarely blazoned. Mostly they are small tasks to continue discovery, knowing it is part of a completely purposeful path.

When the insights reveal the purpose of your work, it becomes more challenging. As heartwarming as it may literally be to see what's possible, the next steps are not always so clear. Most times, when I encounter this type of revelation, I share it with my team and together we brainstorm as to what's next. Sometimes you won't know what's next and the revelation seems like merely a reminder that your work is purposeful and full of possibly. In these cases, the revelation is not merely a reminder. In actuality the tangible action you must take is one of patience. Yes, waiting is part of this game too, there will be what feels like lulls of time that are necessary for other pieces to fall in place. Be patient and know it's all intentional, enjoy and appreciate the calm parts of the journey.

CHAPTER TWELVE

TUNING-IN ON INDIVIDUAL FREQUENCIES

In *The HR Intuitive*, I was fully transparent about my experiences as an empath. It was this empathic nature that caused the life events from my first book, *From Heart to HRart*, to be overwhelming and intense. However, the empathic sense was only part of the equation. Beyond feeling what others were feeling as if the emotions were my own, I also encountered the other individual's energetic field.

It is when our energetic fields come together that we experience the magic of team dynamics and culture formations. Outside the workplace, it is this effortless action of one's energy interacting with another that sparks romance, friendship, and adversaries. In fact, the emotions generated are a result of the energetic mingle, often without conscious intention. Instead, it is best to think of the emotion as a mere reaction to a combination of ultra-complex compounds mixing, sometimes like water and sugar—sweet—other times like water and salt—salty—but know that it can also be like water and oil… where it simply cannot mix.

While learning how to conduct an organizational reading, you were introduced to reading individual energies as well as collective energies of teams and cultures. Now I want to dive deeper and share with you how tuning-in can be beneficial for tangible interventions with both individuals and teams.

A Team is a Collective Whole

Let's begin by addressing working with team energies, since we tend to begin there, rather than at the individual level. My guess is this comes from the belief that team interventions are more efficient, so it makes sense to attempt to address the masses first. However, to make this intervention effective, you must always recognize that a team is a collective whole. Therefore, to make the whole team intervention productive, we must facilitate and navigate individual collective energies to the end goal.

This means you as the practitioner and guide are tasked with conducting the equivalent of an organizational reading for the entire intervention while actively implementing what you are receiving. Therefore, all my slow step-by-steps are now squished into a specific time duration, which I hope brings fresh perspective when working with a leader who demands that team dynamics be fixed within an hour.

The ADDIE Model

"The ADDIE Model, developed by Florida State University in the 1970s, is the most well-known framework for designing instruction to improve human performance. ADDIE is an acronym representing the five key stages of the instructional design process: Analysis, Design, Development, Implementation, and Evaluation.[13]"

For our purposes, I would like to use ADDIE to create the framework needed to facilitate a productive team intervention. Before we dive into the steps, let's take a moment to define *team intervention*. A team intervention is a designed team event that aims to shift the group's capability to perform at the next level. There are four common levels all teams move through, initially identified by Bruce Tuckman in 1965. He referred to them as the four stages of team development, which in sequential order are: *Forming*, *Storming*, *Norming,* and *Performing*. These stages will serve as a baseline for our first step in the adapted ADDIE framework to design a team intervention.

---

[13] https://www.devlinpeck.com/posts/addie-instructional-design

Analysis

During analysis, the primary objective is to obtain as much transparency as possible regarding the team, attempting to understand current dynamics and variables that may be causing challenging conditions. To obtain this information, you should conduct an organizational reading as introduced in the previous chapter. The scope of that reading will focus strictly on any stakeholders surrounding this team. Therefore, it should include at least a site visit, a general interaction with the team, as well as an individual discussion with the supervisor. You might find after completing these actions that your insights suggest further investigation into other organizational elements, such as additional management, policies, or supporting departments.

Before proceeding to the next step, you need to have sufficient information to confidently identify the team's active developmental phase.

- *Forming*: Team members are actively attempting to learn where they belong in the team. Despite how long the team has been working together, whenever a new member is introduced, they are instantly reset to this stage. At this phase, team members lack authenticity and trust because they are unsure of where they stand with their colleagues. In addition, the underlying tone that carries this team has not been established as safe for them to express any level of vulnerability.

- *Storming*: In this second phase of team development, the team is now testing boundaries with the organization and each other. This is innately done to establish roles of how this team will function together. However, it is during this phase that conflict is highly active, and cliques may form. If a team is not guided through their developmental *storm*, they are left to make their own conclusions. These conclusions should ideally be made as a collective, but often are made individually or semi-collective, resulting in an incessant cycle of storming. This stage can turn volatile for a team as it is a common stage for stagnation that, if left unaddressed, can remain for years.

Often, when approached with what others refer to as a "challenging team," you will find you are being invited to intervene with a team that has been trapped in their storm for years. An obvious cause to this lost-at-sea scenario is the absence of leadership. A team's leader is a vital member and should not be treated as a separate entity. They must develop with the team, and during the storming phase their ability to find their established role is critical for forward movement.

- *Norming*: In this phase, the team has finally established norms for how they will function. Conflicts present currently are less about testing each other and are productive in nature, regardless of their juvenile appearance. These conflicts are driven by an intention to further establish a bond, surfacing misunderstandings that have previously been cleared. This is the first stage where team members have expressed a willingness to be vulnerable and signs of a safe underlying tone can be observed. It is common to witness this transition during an intervention, when you have a team in storming that is on the cusp of entering this phase.

At this phase, any assistance provided to create greater clarity and confidence regarding how the team is functioning will be appreciated. It is important to embrace this time to solidify bonds that have been created as well as the perfect primer to share the vision of what they are capable of together.

- *Performing*: Teams at this phase will have an undeniable collective energy that reflects a micro-culture within the greater organizational culture. This will be evident not only through interactions with the team but also reflected in tangible organizational measurements. At this stage, you can provide an intervention that introduces new tools or skills to expand their capabilities through growth. It is also important to know that this is the stage where most leaders mistakenly believe their team is. Therefore, they will request that your time with them focus on growth. Yet, if the team is not yet in their fourth stage of development the intervention will be ineffective as well as potentially jeopardizing to your credibility, impacting your ability to aid the team in the future.

Design

The second step in planning for a productive team intervention is to determine the objective and scope. To achieve this, we will utilize the popular SMART goal acronym. SMART stands for *Specific, Measurable, Achievable, Realistic,* and *Timely.* These are the components to create an actionable goal. In terms of your team intervention, it is important to determine what can logically be achieved. This determination is based on your findings from the assessment process conducted in the analysis phase.

When designing a training intervention, the designer often leaves the scope or objectives too broad. Rather than identifying what will be achieved at the end of the intervention, they instead identify the vision for the outcome that all stakeholders desire. Doing this creates unrealistic expectations for your intervention to stakeholders. The reality is that what you will be able to achieve in this intervention will be a micro-shift in the team's development. The growth journey for team cannot be effectively taken in leaps. It is more of a shuffle that at times requires a step back or repetition. Utilizing the SMART acronym with a modified perspective will allow you to articulate the realistic and appropriate objective for that team's development.

- *Specific*: Your objective for the team intervention must be detailed. It should be an action item. For example, if I have a team that is in storming and, as a result of my analysis, I determine that what is needed is an added layer of transparency amongst team members, a possible specific action item could be to create an opportunity for team members to be transparent with each other. It might sound too simple, however, this level of clarity allows you to isolate your focus on achieving this action. Also, it is important to note that achieving an objective of this nature will require a collection of facilitated activities to create the environment where this type of interaction can occur.

- *Measurable*: Your objective must be measurable, which means there is a clear method to determine when you have achieved it. To continue with the transparency example, the objective can be measured because we can observe when the team members express a level of transparency with each other. Perhaps, this could be benchmarked with team members' sharing feelings that they have only shared with you and not openly with each other. Sometimes we get caught up in the concept of measurability, believing it needs to be a test. However, observation is a powerful tool for evaluation. Sometimes we also believe that for it to be measurable, it must also be obvious to the learner that they are being evaluated. Not true. When it comes to whether an objective is measurable or not, the measurement tool is solely for you. It is a resource for you to determine that the intervention was successful, and the objective was achieved.

- *Achievable* and *Realistic*: These two go together because they make a significant point that needs to be reiterated with two descriptors. Your objective must be something you can achieve during your facilitated intervention. View this portion of the SMART acronym as a helpful checkpoint, to ensure that you are not creating objectives that are more visionary rather than practical. It is also this element that allows you to establish reasonable expectations with the stakeholder who requested the intervention. It is these initial expectations that set the stage for allowing the work to continue past this intervention and materialize true growth for the team while moving toward the desired vision. Long story short, if your objective is not something you can tangibly achieve during your facilitated intervention, then it needs to be revisited.

- *Timely*: Finally, the objective must be able to be met in the physical duration of time that you have for the intervention. There are several initial objectives that are undeniably appropriate recommendations based on your findings in the analysis phase. Regardless, if that objective is what the team needs developmentally, if it cannot be achieved in your allotted amount of time, it needs to be adjusted. It may be helpful to think of that objective as one that can be met by a series of smaller objectives. Take the first of these micro-objectives and use it as the basis for your team intervention design. I am a huge believer that if you have identified what the team truly needs, then advocate for the time you need. Just know, that we are never able to control time. We cannot make it go faster, slower, or bring it to a halt, so your team intervention goal needs to be just right for the time allotted.

Develop

It is during this third step that you finally do what most people begin with—creating the actual sequence of activities you will facilitate during the team intervention. The objectives and scope identified in the previous step should be your guide when selecting activities relevant for your intervention. Every minute of your intervention should be orchestrated with the intentionality of meeting your identified objectives. When facilitating team interventions, choosing to include activities that are disconnected from the scope has the ability to detract from the entire experience.

With that being said, our filter for what activities are meaningful and productive is often drastically off base. Our perspective on adult education and training has been molded by individuals who lack expertise in this area. Therefore, we automatically discard valid activities, classifying them as unproductive and a waste of valuable time. Yet, because we decide not to use these activities we become unable to meet our objectives. Sometimes activities that are perceived wastes of time serve to break down barriers and build trust that is an absolute essential primer for a team to move forward.

I propose that we adjust our lenses. Bob Pike is my idol in the training world, and he is a mastermind when it comes to creating engaging participant-centered training. He names Five Laws of

Adult Learning, and these laws can help guide you when considering what to include in your intervention facilitation plan. [14]

Law 1: Adults Are Babies in Big Bodies

Upon entering the workforce many of us have discovered that the workplace is filled with social interactions that mimic high school. In fact, I believe this illustrates the significance of the social element in youth education. If you take a moment and look around, especially if you are navigating conflict-infested waters, you may realize that the individuals involved are acting in a "child-like fashion."

I place that phrase in quotes because child-like characteristics have developed a negative association. However, the presence of child-like characteristics demonstrates a willingness to be authentic and vulnerable. This could be for one of two reasons. The first is that the workplace culture has provided a sufficient safe space for individuals to reveal their authentic vulnerable nature. Therefore, regardless that the culture is not in its ideal state, this revelation hints at a pretty good condition and should be a cause for reassurance as you prepare for your intervention.

The second provides quite an opposite scenario, that the workplace culture was once safe but has now become so toxic that it has pushed individuals to their limits where they have no choice but to break down and expose this authentic vulnerable nature. In this scenario, the individuals will be entering the intervention in a fragile state. Keep in mind that the workplace culture once provided a safe opportunity for them to be vulnerable and can do that once again. However, the most recent experience is that when they were vulnerable, they were taken advantage of or exposed in a way that caused deep shame or anger.

When these child-like characteristics are observed, it is easy to understand why implementing Pike's Law of Babies in Big Bodies

---

[14] https://www.bobpikegroup.com/trainer-blog/creative-training-techniques-101-the-basics

is needed. However, you may find yourself surrounded my individuals lacking emotions altogether. This neutral, cold exterior with limited reaction is the result of a workplace culture that has never provided a safe space for authenticity. Therefore, underneath this hard exterior is still the child-like authenticity and vulnerability waiting for a safe space to emerge.

I share all this to say that you cannot go wrong when embracing this Pike Law. It does not literally translate to engaging with your team as if you were cooing at a baby, but it does ask that you facilitate activities which would entice a child and be easily understood. This law should eliminate any grand activities that are too complex in nature. Instead, emphasize simplicity—think beach balls, coloring, and jeopardy.

Law 2: People Don't Argue with Their Own Data

There is a weird assumption that we have accepted openly with limited resistance in our culture, that to train or teach another we must know everything. This couldn't be further from the truth. In fact, those who are called to teach and train can often universally agree that learning and teaching are one in the same. We learn when we teach, and when we teach others learn. It is a cyclical cycle that creates an essential collaboration for education to occur.

Furthermore, we feed this false assumption by designing training that requires us to be all-knowing, magnifying the pressure and likelihood of failure. Even worse, a successful delivery of this design often leads to the takeover of a misaligning ego that can potentially derail the work entirely.

The answer to counteract this type of design is simple. Instead of being all-knowing, view your role as strictly a guide who must provide only the framework for learning. The specific data, experiences, and how everything materializes can be provided by those participating. This is a win-win by increasing participant engagement directly and drastically decreasing participant resistance—their experience and knowledge is essentially embedded into the design. Not only is it embedded, but it is also recognized and inevitably allows the participant to feel valued for their contribution.

To achieve this, these types of activities include discussion questions where you inquire directly about others' experiences, group sharing exercises, and even journaling. This also includes leaving intentional space for flexibility. If a topic of discussion is presented by a participant that is relevant to your ultimate objective, it is important to be able to allow time for this detour that might prove more effective than anything you had previously planned.

Law 3: Learning is Directly Proportional to the Amount of Fun You Have

One of the major clues that participants are having fun is laughter. Laughter and even fun are often categorized as borderline inefficient; social interaction is often viewed as a time waster. However, what is being achieved by the act of laughter is monumental for our purposes.

A study in 2006, found that even anticipation of laughter helps "positive psychological mood states" and decreases stress as proven by measuring cortisol levels in the bloodstream.[15] In addition, the act of laughter involves the whole brain rather than just one hemisphere, we need the right and left side to achieve our best work.

"One study experimented with the electrical activity that occurs when we laugh. 'About four-tenths of a second after we hear the punch line of a joke—but before we laugh—a wave of electricity sweeps through the cortex,' reports Peter Derks, a professor of psychology at the College of William and Mary. [16]" This means before you even hear laughter you are activating the brain. When it comes to corporate training and interventions, we tend to enter the space as participants prepared only to engage with half of our mind.

---

[15] https://www.sciencedaily.com/releases/2008/04/080407114617 .htm

[16] https://thethirty.whowhatwear.com/what-happens-to-your-brain-when-you-laugh

The left hemisphere of the brain controls speech, comprehension, arithmetic, and writing—all skills we have come to expect in training and even traditional educational environments. However, the right hemisphere of the brain possesses our potential to tap into creativity, imagination, intuition, and emotions. The right side governs the aspects of the brain we need to shift perspective and obtain buy-in.

Law 4: Learning Has Not Taken Place Until Behavior Has Changed

We will discuss this law in greater detail when we unpack the final step in the ADDIE Model. However, regarding design, this law poses the question of, "What must we do to witness the change?" Often the response is not isolated to the defined timed intervention but instead presents an opportunity for follow-up. This is the chance to create an avenue to determine if the intervention was successful. It is also another friendly check on your intervention objectives. If your scope is too hefty, it will be challenging to answer the question of how or when you could witness the change in the group.

This law also adds a realistic check to the duration necessary for the work to get done. Remember that your intervention might be a baby shuffle in the right direction. It would be wise for you to look at the potential timeline this work may actually take to obtain the change needed within this team. This realistic evaluation is not only needed for establishing expectations with other stakeholders but also allows you to anticipate the impact this timeline might have on the organization overall.

Law 5: Fu Yu, Wu Yu, Wzu Tu Yu

This final law sounds like gibberish. Pike's rough translation of this phrase is, "Mama's having it, or Papa's having it, ain't like Baby having it." Continuing with our theme regarding children, this law reminds us that as the authority figure in the intervention design, just because you deem an activity or even an objective significant, it does not mean your participants will agree. This is an evolved version of the popular WII-FM mentality, urging us to tune into our participants by remembering *What's In It For Me?* Your design must answer this question for every participant. Why must they care about the intervention and its outcomes? What happens if they don't care or enter the space half-heartedly? The why, both individually and collectively, is the essence of a team intervention, and without it, resistance is inevitable.

Implement

The fourth phase is the act of facilitating the team intervention. Therefore, I would like to take this opportunity to review a few facilitation strategies that can also be used for individual coaching or one-on-one work. As mentioned earlier, one of the key successes to implementing a team intervention comes from your ability to read and navigate the individual and collective energies that are present.

When it comes to team inventions, the goal is to create a collective energy that is harmonious. In order to achieve this, you need to address any energies that deviate from the group's energy. Those deviated energies will vary from person to person throughout the intervention as the design is implemented. Each activity that you intentionally place into the design will cause individuals to be triggered at different times. Sometimes it is the same individual over and over, however most of the time it will be divided equally among the group. If you find yourself in a situation where only one individual is consistently deviating, this is a strong indicator that a team intervention might not have been necessary but instead individual coaching might have been more appropriate.

In fact, if you realize this is the case, you might consider pausing the intervention altogether and share transparently your new belief that the intervention is no longer the best way to proceed. Choosing to continue when you know it is only one individual's energy that is causing the disharmony will be challenging, because the WII-FM for the remaining group members will be hard to establish. This once again reiterates the significance of your initial assessment before ever agreeing to proceed with facilitating a team intervention.

Facilitation Strategy #1: Tune into One

The act of reading the group's energy is fairly like the method we utilized to conduct an organizational reading. The major difference here is that we want to recognize the collective energy while also taking a moment to tune into each individual. The best way to achieve this is to arrive early and take a moment to personally greet each team member. This provides the opportunity for you to spend time solely in that individual's energy and recognize what they are bringing to the group. It is also beneficial to pay attention to how the individuals enter the space after you greet them. Do they instantly gravitate toward others? Do they remain aloof or appear distracted? Take the opportunity to witness the collective energy build and settle in a group dynamic.

Facilitation Strategy #2: The Icebreaker Test

The popular ice breaker activity is often encouraged to literally break the ice and allow the participants to let down their guard and begin engaging. However, I encourage the use of this activity for a different reason. Opening group exercises—no matter how silly in nature—allow you to observe the team in a collective fashion. Doing this at the start of your team intervention provides the benefit of quickly identifying the major outlying energies. These energies often materialize during ice breaker exercises as resistance, closed off non-verbal language, heavy sarcasm, pessimism, or cliques.

The key to ensuring an ice breaker will serve as beneficial is that it must be an activity that requires the team to function as a group. Therefore, activities that include simple introductions will not provide the dynamic involvement necessary to witness the group's energy at play. The most instrumental activities for this purpose will be ones that encourage the group to interact in different ways with different people as well as with a varying number of people. For example, I am a huge fan of an activity that begins with two people working together, then that partner works with another set of partners before moving to large-group sharing.

It is also important to consider that if you are aware of clique-like behaviors or intergroup conflicts, you might want to control how the group activity specifically plays out. You can do this by creating initial partner assignments or even creating nametags that lay out an intentional seating chart. I caution you to only utilize this tactic if you know undoubtedly it will serve the group. There is a large amount of value in allowing adults to have a choice during a team intervention design, as it plays in your favor of limiting resistance. Therefore, I often encourage the power of choice where possible, unless there is a high need to observe certain individuals together.

Facilitation Strategy #3: Follow Distraction

This third and final facilitation strategy, is what I frequently use when coaching individuals or in my one-on-one work. It involves simply following the distraction. In a group setting, energies that are deviating will display as distracting. Therefore, when someone becomes a distraction to you, it is because they are out of harmony with the group. The question then becomes, "What do we do to bring them back into harmony?" This depends on whether the distraction manifests tangibly or intangibly.

Let's begin by discussing the tangible distractions. This could be someone having side conversations constantly during the session, working on a laptop, playing on their phone, or taking frequent breaks where they are missing for a long duration. If you have been working on your own personal cultivation, you may be able to shift the energy by merely presenting your own. You can do this by changing your facilitation position to be directly near the individual who is deviating from the group. For this to work, you must be at least 2-3 feet from the individual. If you find that presenting your energy triggers this individual further, it is likely that one-on-one work will be needed. Acknowledging this will transition your objective to minimizing their distraction to others, as well as providing permission to move on to the next distracting energy source.

If you have doubts that your energy is at a place where it can elevate others, then I encourage you to directly address the tangible distraction. This should be completed during a break with a one-on-one conversation, rather than in the group. During this conversation, share with the individual how their current actions are impacting the team's ability to grow together, making sure to be specific by naming the distracting actions. If the source for the tangible distraction comes from an individual possessing a belief that they cannot step away from their work for the intervention, this speaks to an obstacle that must be addressed with the supervisory stakeholders. If the messaging from above regarding this intervention does not signal significance and priority, it will be hard to sustain buy-in and maximize effectiveness.

More frequently, the distractions will materialize as intangible. This means they manifest as a feeling or thought that often appears random—random enough that we mistake it for our own distraction and can easily push it to the side. Instead, it is important to pause when we get this random feeling or thought that presents itself and identify the source individual. As you set the intention to enter the space to facilitate change in the group's collective energy, you are automatically hooked up to "see" what needs to be seen to do your work. This "seeing" includes random feelings and thoughts. It is the intangible distractions that I use most in my one-on-one work. I find there is always an intangible distraction present. It is just in a group setting that those which are out of alignment will appear more pressing or obvious. As they clear, it will make space for the next intangible distraction needing attention.

To clear an intangible distraction, you merely need to identify and bring it to the surface with a level of curiosity. Even though you have identified who is the source of the distraction, calling them out specifically is not necessary. You can use the information from the distraction to service the rest of the group. Sometimes it is the way others in the group will respond to the information presented that will clear the distraction without the source having to directly engage. For example, if a random thought that comes to mind is your family, this might prompt a question to the group like, "How does what we are talking about impact your relationship with your families?"

It is this phase that establishes the case for why prior preparation and design for team interventions is so important. If you are caught up in what you are physically doing next, you will be unable to sustain the capacity to be present at the level to notice the subtleties for powerful intangible distractions.

Evaluate

The final phase of ADDIE happens after the team intervention has concluded. Immediately afterward, take a moment and log all your observations. When possible, I opt for a facilitation partner, which empowers you to log observations while the intervention is in progress. Plus, during times when you are not physically leading, there is an opportunity to observe which only greatly assists your ability to navigate the collective energies. Most times, it will not be possible to have a partner, so consider making space in your design for observation. How can you create activities that requires you physically doing less so you can spend more time discerning?

Once you have logged all your observations and insights from the intervention, allow the information to sit for at least a day and possibly even as long as a week before attempting to truly debrief what occurred. This may feel like procrastination, but I have come to recognize it as a "marination" on what was at work. After this pause, revisit your log with fresh eyes, seeking to uncover the most potent points. These points could be shifts that you witnessed. They could also include key items that were revealed that explain why the team experiences minimal growth. Use these points to build an action item list for follow-up. Be prepared to discover that your work here has only begun, and be grateful for all that the intervention revealed.

CHAPTER THIRTEEN

THE NEEDED RESILIENCY

By definition, the word resiliency is a noun that describe our capacity to recover from difficulties. When I was only five years into my career as an HR Practitioner, I found myself hitting a wall. In only a short time, my capacity to recover after countless obstacles was gone. More importantly, my hope of making a difference within an organization seemed to have died as well. When it comes to the world of HR, I have found that the truly passionate practitioners in this field rely heavily on the concept of "making a difference." As cheesy as it may sound, there is an initial ambition instilled in them to make the working world a better place. When that ambition is slowly dismantled, we lose the very substance necessary to keep getting up and trying again.

It was this exact circumstance that caused me to submit my one-month resignation with an organization that I had initially dreamed I would one day retire from. In addition, my resignation was not so I could pursue a greener pasture, but rather to reevaluate my life completely. It was after a month of reflection that I found myself entering the field again, but only under the terms of training. I found hope in the training and development function of HR, believing that perhaps it could be the path for me to make a difference.

What I didn't realize at that exact moment was that I was experiencing the innate calling to engage in the healing art that has been missing from leadership. For the first five years of my career, I witnessed suffering and learned to build a hard exterior—an exterior my mentors told me I needed to keep the work from devouring my soul. I was taught how to numb and disconnect so that some aspect of the work could be left behind rather than carried incessantly.

This reality was affirmed when I began teaching business students at a local college. As we dove into the concepts of what HR Management is meant to be in the workplace and how it should function, I was taken back by the students as they experienced genuine surprise about the power of this business function. It also provided an additional platform for me to hear about more workplace suffering and what it's like for an employee to experience an HR Practitioner's armor. One student shared in a paper reflecting on her past experiences with HR that, "the lack of a good HR department left a bad taste in my soul." This statement describes beautifully the resistance we experience in transforming the workplace, but also the intimacy we are able to tap into. No other business function speaks directly to the soul.

In HR, every action and decision we make is part of an unwritten but known contract with the people who work there. This contract is created the day we begin recruitment and is further affirmed when we select and offer employment. In a way, we build the foundation for why an individual should choose and trust our organization. That's why, when a decision of action appears to be out of character for what you promised, it feels like an act of betrayal. Despite the heavy burden, it is also this level of responsibility that enables you to sustain an engaged workforce. It paints a clear picture why those organizations without a functional capable department struggle desperately to retain and sustain minimal engagement. How quick and easy it is to disengage from work when you believe there is no one there who cares!

In this final chapter, I want to share with you two major variables regarding this healing work and integrating it into your practice. First, I want to speak to each of our major HR functions and add the energetic component that underlies each one. It is its absence that has resulted in our effectiveness being so limited. Then, I want to share with you how to remain resilient while doing this work. As you tackle this work, you will hit walls, you will be knocked down, and therefore you need buoyancy to get up and come again and again. You will also need to be able to do this without depleting yourself completely.

C is for Competency

Competency models identify what it takes for an individual to be successful in a position or role. When it comes to the HR profession there are two recognized competency models—the SHRM and HRCI Model. For our purposes, we will speak about both models rather than focusing on just one. This is because I believe both models are justified in some capacity. In fact, I believe that when SHRM released their competency model it was an attempt to explain the energetic navigation we all know is present in our profession but are unsure of how to identify. This might also be why the competency model received such heavy criticism upon release, because it claimed to measure a skillset that is so intangible.

If we take a step back, we will see that these models actually provide a mini-HR history lesson and outline the evolution of the profession. With that perspective in mind, I'd like to take the competencies presented by both models and classify them into three evolutionary phases.

The Classic Phase

This phase encompasses what I have come to call the HR classics. It is the core body of knowledge that, due to the state of our current working world, we must know. This includes Risk Management, Employee and Labor Relations, as well as Compensation and Benefits, predominantly driven by limiting risk in compliance with federal, state, and local legislation. This has become the standard for how HR provides value to the organization.

The Defensive Phase

The SHRM Competency Model introduced many skillsets for success that were strictly reactionary. Therefore, instead of identifying competencies from a place of vision of what our profession could be, they were identified from a place of reacting to our current state of industry and what we need to be to combat current stereotypes. Competencies models always aim at addressing an identified gap by becoming the bridge to get from point A to B, therefore what is identified as point B is significant. The high number of defensive-like competencies hints at a desire to attempt to fit in rather than maximize our true capabilities.

This phase includes Business Acumen, Critical Evaluation, Leadership & Navigation, and HR Technology. Do not misunderstand me. I do recognize these competencies as significant to the success of an organization, however the motive as to why they are included in an HR Competency Model is most likely rooted in years of heavy criticism regarding HR failing to deliver in these areas. They also happen to be areas that our operational counterparts have the highest probability of understanding, so therefore it provides a platform to pass judgment and make assumptions.

The Origins Phase

This phase includes competencies to address root causes that we have now identified that generated our current state. For example, the source for why employment law or labor unions were needed includes competencies of Global & Cultural Effectiveness and Ethical Practice.

The Four HR Intuitive Competencies

If you are familiar with these competency models, you may have noticed that not all their components were mentioned. The remaining pieces are what I believe make up the key areas where energetic navigation skills are necessary. They will assist us in defining the four HR Intuitive competencies of *Crystal*, *Consciousness*, *Collective*, and *Cultivation*.

Crystal

In the world of business, there are several times when we invent new terms to reference classic definitions. I would be lying if I didn't admit that this is a personal pet peeve… why make a classic more complicated or confusing? However, now I'm going to bite my tongue as I do the exact same thing with this competency. In a perfect world, this competency would retain its classical name of *clarity*, but in today's world the term needs an upgrade so it can once again be noticed and respected as the powerful skill it is. For decades, we have taken clarity for granted, believing we have it all figured out because we partake in periodic business planning retreats, and actively have a mission and vision statement.

When it comes to HR, the base criteria we have been using for clarity establishes a clear case for why it needs to be revisited. The mission and vision statements often reflect a disconnection from organizational culture. The amount of dissonance varies from employees not aware of how their work connects to the statements to complete irrelevance of the statements to the work that is actually occurring within the organization.

I intentionally chose this awkward term of *crystal* because of its obvious imagery. It implies transparency, where all the work that pertains to this competency has a shared understanding for all organizational stakeholders. In fact, if we can break it down further, let's imagine a literal piece of crystal-like glass, representing our mission, vision, and any other major organizational decisions. As leaders, creators, and decision-makers we stand on one side of the glass. Our employees, those with limited access to the creation and decision process, stand on the other. Both parties, should be able to look clearly through the glass with a crystal-clear understanding of how the outcome was generated.

For this reason, I directly link the business and strategy management components of the SHRM and HRCI competency models to this HR Intuitive Competency. From an energetic perspective, it is in our capacity to gauge the connection and alignment of strategic work to the people. When a disconnect or misalignment exists, we begin to experience distrust, disengagement, and overall drama in our organizations. It is our ability to gauge the level of connection and alignment that provides the opportunity for the HR Practitioner to serve as a strategic guide to move decisions in a universally productive direction.

Consciousness

Consciousness is connected to the SHRM competencies for communication and relationship management. This intuitive competency is strictly focused on being present. The clearing work you completed in Part Two of this book, allows you to have the capacity to be present at the level needed to achieve this competency. Brené Brown explains connection as "the energy that exists between people when they feel seen, heard, and valued; when they can give and receive without judgment; and when they derive sustenance and strength from the relationship."[17] This is the outcome of the conscious competency. It allows us to connect with the people within our workplaces in a way that limits resistance and barriers to make space for harmony and collective momentum. It is this collective momentum that fulfills an organization's mission and makes the vision seem within plausible reach.

The previous chapter focused a great deal on how this competency tangibly materializes while facilitating team interventions and coaching.

Collective

The collective momentum, referenced as an outcome of consciousness, is at the core of the collective competency— collective more so because it provides perspective of how to approach its corresponding SHRM competency of consulting. In the SHRM Model, consulting encompasses problem solving, analytic reasoning, coaching, people, and project management. In a nutshell,

---

[17] Brown, B., *The Gifts of Imperfection*, Hazelden Publishing, 2010.

it is about resolution. When it comes to approaching these tasks, collective encourages us to always take two steps back to ensure we see the whole picture. I use the term "whole" to reference all that matters to the organization. Sometimes we are asked to revisit the bigger picture, which is helpful, yet the term "bigger" asks us to think less of ourselves in sacrifice of a greater service to others, something beyond ourselves. This way of thinking begins to prioritize the significance of humanity based off of role. This dismissing of the human element has resulted in a silent personal rebellion that has materialized as demands often characterized as selfish. It is our ability to look at the whole that gives us the capacity to lead true culture change.

As a consultant, I frequently receive quick-fix culture calls. These typically come from non-HR leaders, sharing that they have recently learned of a morale issue among staff and need it fixed. From their viewpoint, this issue should be able to be resolved by an all-staff meeting where there is an opportunity for transparent communication that then magically generates some sort of cultural reset and all is well.

This meeting concept is an accurate starting point, however the objective of them is not resolution yet a tool to grasp the whole picture. When I receive these calls, I can't help but return to memories of my Lean Leader Training, where my instructors constantly yelled, "Go to the Gemba!" Gemba is a Japanese word meaning "the actual place" and in Lean they use it to reference "the place where the value is created." In the world of HR, the Gemba will always be where the people are.

Therefore, since these meeting are essentially a Gemba, I agree to assist. These initial meetings provide me a window to explore if there is a genuine possibility to materialize change within that specific work environment. Many times, during the facilitation of these meetings, I receive confused non-verbal feedback. On the fact that I spend most of my time listening rather than speaking or sharing my insights. This frustration comes from a lack of understanding of the energetic components at play for an initial meeting of this nature to occur successfully. It is our capacity to sustain consciousness that creates a safe space for the transparent communication to occur in a healthy productive fashion.

At the conclusion of these meetings, it is often expected that the outcome is a list of small action items that address every specific concern presented. While this certainly is one follow-up approach to the feedback received, it will ultimately be limited in impact.

The collective competency speaks to our ability to look at the feedback as symptoms of a root cause that is negatively impacting the wellness of the whole organization. Our skillset is in identifying the root and addressing it, accordingly, causing ripple resolutions for the symptoms. This competency is achieved when we can withstand the push back for our approach to look at the whole and find methods to act to address the root issue. It is within our capacity to know what is possible once the root issue is healed. It is this visionary capability that I believe is key to unlocking organizational performance that we have yet to observe.

Cultivation

The word cultivate is often used when referencing crops or gardening. In that context, the word describes preparing the land for use. This competency corresponds with the SHRM and HRCI competencies of workforce planning and human resource development. These HR functions focus on preparing the workforce. In an ideal world, these functions would be more future-oriented, rather than strictly utilized for immediate needs.

Our lack of workforce planning became overwhelmingly clear as we navigated a global pandemic in 2020. We experienced a wake-up call, regarding the amount of excess we had in our work processes, which generated an initial wave of layoffs as we realized essential positions indeed could do a bit more with some workflow adjustments. We also witnessed organizations scramble as the reality sunk in that they had little to no flexibility with their staffing model. As fear of leaving the home set in for many, these organizations were at a loss for how they would fill positions that they could not function without. Both scenarios inevitably were the perfect storm for disengagement; the only difference was that one scenario was correcting while the other was actively generating.

The scenario with excess tells of an organization that had over-simplified positions and underestimated their employees. Over-simplified positions eventually become mundane. It is often boredom that drives employees to use their excess time to explore alternatives. These alternatives range from other employment options to the development of internal social practices that become distracting. The second scenario of no flexibility ultimately leads to treadmill syndrome for employees. The longer the vacancies remain, the longer current employees are asked to step up to fill the gap. This equation can only be sustained by an individual for so long before they begin to break. However, the question that arises out of this second scenario is less about the make-up of the positions and more so about why an individual would want to work for the organization.

In the collective competency, I mentioned the silent personal rebellion that is occurring as a result of the incessant push to see the bigger picture. It is this rebellion that has caused us to continually address the WII-FM, What's In It For Me. More so now than ever, recruitment strategies must evolve to consider and cater to this rebellion. This is where cultivation comes in. It is within our capacity to cultivate individuals to become a pivotal component of the workforce planning process. There is a reason we hire humans rather than robots. There is a potential we observe in people every day that instills in us a knowing that the added individualism can change everything for the better. Cultivation is our capacity to see the individuals within our organization and what they are truly capable. Cultivation is our capacity to focus on their growth and maximize their potential. Cultivation is our capacity to know that individualism is essential to organizational greatness.

So Much Is Counterintuitive

My hope is as you read about the HR Intuitive Competencies, that at some level you feel it resonating. A gentle vibration lets you know there are hints of truth in these words. I recognize that an initial reaction could be so stark and with every logical fiber of your being wanting to resist these counter concepts. I was raised in the same corporate society and it took a global pandemic for me to finally see that the current systems are not working. Those who were engaged in their work were not well, and those who were disengaged from their work were lost. These competencies speak to a way of work not yet fully embraced; therefore, I am not even sure what they are fully capable of. What I do know is if you are functioning in any sort of people-driven profession post-2020, then you are as desperate as I am to find the way forward.

In full transparency, you may find yourself being called to take on the Phoenix persona to move the work forward. Part of the reason I stepped into third-party consulting was because I understood the power of shaking trees—someone who could come in, say what needs to be said, do what needs to be done, push, and then step away so the messy evolution could occur. The reality for HR departments-of-one or HR departments-of-none is that a budget for third-party consulting is often non-existent and therefore you find yourself being asked to be that someone. The concept of stepping away is less about fear and more about failure. Those of us who genuinely do the work for the people see leaving as abandoning those they failed. What you need to hear is sometimes your departure is the move that breaks up the overwhelming toxic stagnation to create some sort of motion. Sometimes your first step is what gives those who are clinging to hope the courage to step away as well.

Every year, I have an astrology consultation to learn about what I should anticipate energetically from the stars. If throughout this process you have discovered you are a highly energetic sensitive individual, I highly recommend you do the same. The stars are an entire additional environmental influence that we must consider. During these consultations, my astrologer reminds me of the need to release things that do not serve me as I continue to grow. It is this act of periodic releasing that makes space for inner growth to occur. When I pushed for further guidance, he provided me with the beautiful imagery of the ocean—thinking of life and everything that comes with it as the tide. It comes in and is then carried back out again. We must live in a space where we are always okay to put anything on that wave to be carried out and trust that if it's meant to stay it will be brought right back in. We do not have the capacity to carry the burden of what we need to hold onto at any given moment. Instead, leave that task to the wave, acknowledging the possibility that something greater than your ego knows what's best for you.

Bubble Up for Protection

As you take on this task of pioneering a way of work that might seem foreign to everyone around you, it is important to be reminded of the powerful tool from Part Two. The Bubble Up exercise was used to initially establish boundaries and increase awareness of your sensitivities. You then utilized it again to conduct organizational readings. Now I invite you to use the Bubble Up concept as a means of protection. Whenever you must come in contact with people who do not yet understand the vision, bubble up. Place yourself in a safe space, so that you know where your emotions end and others' begin. This energetic boundary is necessary if you want to continue moving this work forward. When we allow the emotionally charged opinions and thoughts of others to run through us like a high-speed highway, we can easily lose our way. It is the lack of these boundaries that has caused the massive delay in us recognizing the significance of our intuitive capacity. It is also the lack of these boundaries that has drastically limited our intuitive capacity overall.

Conclusion

The Dao of My HRart

It seems so appropriate that we end where we began, completing a circle with newfound clarity, a circle I didn't even know we had started when I first felt the call to share these thoughts as words in written form. I was convinced that I needed to clarify the ending of my first book, *From Heart to HRart*, and establish its place in my work. But now as we conclude this book journey together, what I have gained is finally a genuine understanding of the significance of that earlier work.

If you haven't realized yet by the patterns and reappearing themes, *From Heart to HRart* was a book that bewildered me. After it materialized, I spent years reflecting on its purpose and sometimes even its worth. I was confused at the stories I felt compelled to share as well as my desperation to capture the raw emotion that accompanied them. This obsession to deliver emotions in authentic form reappeared as I wrote *The HR Intuitive*. However, the stories shared in that second volume came from a much different place. The first book was filled with fear, pain, and questions of worthiness, while the second was driven by passion.

To ensure that lessons related to Qigong were accurately portrayed in *The HR Intuitive*, I asked my teacher, Ted O'Brien, for feedback. His words of affirmation also contained a hint of caution. He was concerned that my passion might be misinterpreted by readers as anger. He didn't want the world to know a version of me that was not accurate.

As I sat with his words and concerns, as well as feedback from other early bird readers and editors, I ultimately decided to leave the stories untouched—not because I disagreed with his assessment, but instead because I did agree. My passion for this work was rising out of a place of anger and frustration, one that I had been suppressing and now was overflowing and forcing itself to the surface. Instead of choosing to live as an active volcano on the verge of an unpredictable eruption, I decided to release it all by publishing. The result was that it created space for clarity and the capacity to begin healing others.

These books have captured my beautiful transmutation of energy.

Three Treasures

When you think of treasure, maps with big red x's might come to mind. However, from a Daoist perspective, a long journey to hunt for these precious gems is not necessary. The journey does not require an adventure to some far-off land; what it does require is a look within. You possess three treasures within yourself. These three treasures are *Jing*, *Qi*, and *Shen*.

Jing is our physical form and essence. It is our bodies that serve as our vehicle for this life and it is our Jing that fuels this powerful resource. The source for our Jing lies at the lower abdomen in a space, known as the Lower Dantian.

Qi is our emotional and mental state. It is the processing and transforming hub of the body. The source for our Qi is known as the Middle Dantian, positioned in the chest near the area of the heart.

Shen is our spirit, our connection to the Divine source. It rests in the Upper Dantian, near the crown of the head and third eye.

These three treasures represent the basis of life, and the magic comes in our capacity to transmute them in an artform known as internal alchemy. Daoist internal alchemy speaks to the ultimate goal of "returning to source," utilizing the art and science of gathering, storing, and circulating energy to connect to the Dao.

Self-Cultivation

The path to return to source, is one that requires the transformation of Jing to Qi to Shen as well as the reverse path of Shen to Qi to Jing.

The transformation of Jing to Qi is achieved when we increase our awareness from strictly a physical body to the awareness of energy. Before doing this, it is often necessary to strengthen our Jing, focusing on the physical body. It is when we prepare and care for our physical vessel that we have the capacity to engage in methods to begin transmuting Qi.

Our Qi will begin to elevate to Shen when we are able to transition our awareness from energy to the awareness of the mind. This is accomplished as we care for our energy pathways, cleansing and balancing them. This allows us to nourish our Spirit with Qi. The biggest obstacle to achieving this is our emotions that affect our thinking and upset the balance of our spirit.

It is at the Shen level that we have the ability to move into Wuji, when our awareness shifts from the mind to the awareness of boundless space. From there, we are able to shift from boundless space to the awareness of the Dao, our way.

Daoist Alchemy and the Corporate World

Daoist Internal Alchemy plays a significant role in the current obstacles we face in the workplace from an organizational cultural perspective. There is a reason I believe that HR practitioners and people-driven leaders are called now to serve as workplace healers. That reason lies in what could be possible when an organizational leader could masterfully move from Jing to Shen and Shen to Jing. This individual would be connected to a clarity that is much bigger, that would serve us as a collective whole, rather than rooted in short-minded visioning as acts of survival.

Let's take a moment and recognize the common ways we have been obstructing the transmuting of Jing to Qi to Shen. At the Jing level, we are actively not caring for our bodies, whether it is what we put into them, expose them to, or what we choose to use them for. Our workplace norms consist of happy hours, elaborate dinners with decadent desserts, and sedentary functions. At the Qi level, we are taught from an early age not to cry and then ingrained that emotions are unprofessional in the workplace. At the Shen level, we are unable to let go of emotional-driven thought and obsessive thinking. This is the everyday working world for so many.

If we were able to empower individuals to move away from reaction to intention-driven work, what would be possible? What would we each be capable of?

As a healer, our ability to transform Jing to Qi to Shen, speaks to our personal transformation and healing. However, I believe it is when we are able to master the reverse path of Shen to Qi to Jing that we are able to aid others in their personal transformation. This reverse path enables us to take our connection to the Divine and transform it back into a tangible manifestation that may be shared.

As Dr. Jerry Alan Johnson shares, he was taught the ultimate goal is "to awaken those who are energetically and spiritually asleep, and to apprentice those who are already awake."

A Library Apprenticeship

My books have captured this transition of Jing-level work (in *From Heart to HRart*) to Qi-level work (in *The HR Intuitive*). As I continue working at the Qi level, I have begun to see hints of Shen and what's possible. My hope is that these words I have written over the last five years have instilled in you a recognition that you are already awake. Along with this realization, if you love people the way I do in the workplace, you also now know the work is just getting started.

Our workplaces have been energetically and spiritually sleeping for way too long and it's time to awaken the potential and possibility. The future depends on workplace healers stepping up to answer the call and bringing the Dao to Human Resources.

HR Healer

Toolkit

CHAPTER FOURTEEN

TOOLS FOR WORKPLACE HEALING
by Samm Smeltzer

On the following pages you will find a curated collection of resources. They are formatted in a fashion to be easy to reference, to allow you to quickly move to action without too much of a deep dive into why it is essential or effective. If you need to be reminded of the philosophy or intention behind any of these resources, please reference the corresponding chapter in the book.

I have selected these resources as a mixture of easy reference guides for what you have already learned and are beginning to implement, as well as additional helpful aids from myself and a few friends on topics where they are able to provide further guidance.

It's time to move forward and begin this healing work.

Inside this chapter you will find:

1. Quiet the Monkey Mind

2. Creating a Healing State

3. Visiting a Past Workplace Ghost

4. Releasing What Does Not Serve Me

5. Where Do They Live

6. The Soul's Spark

7. The Foundational Formula

8. No Minimum Obligation Connected Check-Ins

9. Conducting an Organizational Reading

10. Designing a Team Intervention

11. Power Resume Design

12. Inner Purpose Mediation

1. Quiet the Monkey Mind

Objective: Recognize and settle the thoughts of things to do, what-if scenario processing and our desire to always remain in control.

1. Settle in and breathe.

2. Notice and take stock of your internal distractions.

3. Acknowledge each thought, feeling, and sensations that presents itself, then ask it to step aside.

4. Continue until all present thoughts, feelings, and sensations have been recognized.

2. Creating a Healing State

Objective: Open your mind's eye to prepare for your healing work.

1. Quiet the Monkey Mind to find a state of stillness.

2. Deepen the breath to journey inward.

3. Ask your inner self, "where am I?"

4. Take in the landscape that materializes and surrounds you.

5. To return, focus on breath and awaken the body slowly.

3. Visiting a Past Workplace Ghost

Objective: Revisit lessons of previous workplaces that are unresolved.

1. Quiet the Monkey Mind to find a state of stillness.

2. Allow your mind to wander to workplaces of the past.

3. Ask your inner self, "Where was I?"

4. Take stock of everything that begins to materialize.

5. Once the visit is complete, focus on breath and awaken the body slowly.

6. Capture your visit observations and curiosities.

4. Releasing What Does Not Serve Me

Objective: Retain unleashed wisdom and release suppressed toxic emotions.

1. Begin Natural Breathing.

2. Inhale while silently saying, I breathe in healing energy. Restore me and serve my highest good.

3. Exhale through the mouth, while silently saying, I release all that does not serve me.

4. Accompany the exhale with a sigh or corresponding healing sound, if desired.

5. Once you have experienced the release, begin to awaken the body slowly.

Grief	shhh, sss
Anger	shu (shoo)
Anxiety	haa
Doubt	whoo, hooo (hoe)
Fear	yuuu (you)

5. Where Do They Live

Objective: Identify where a recurring emotion lives in the body.

1. Begin Natural Breathing.
2. Focus on the emotion you identified, explore it with further curiosity.
3. Provide permission for your inner self to answer using imagery and sensations.
4. Magnify sensations being experienced in the body.
5. Isolate sensations being experienced in the body and identify where they are located.
6. Once clear on the sensations and their locations, begin to awaken the body.
7. Capture your experiences.

6. The Soul's Spark

Objective: Reconnect to what is truly possible for you.

1. Begin Natural Breathing.

2. Allow a mirror to materialize in your mind's eye, creating your reflection.

3. Gaze into your reflection's eyes.

4. Withdraw from the eyes and take notice of the younger version of presents.

5. Engage in play with your younger self.

6. Say goodbye to your younger self.

7. Begin to awaken the body.

8. Capture the feeling and physical sensation experienced while engaging in play.

7. The Foundational Formula

Objective: Design your personal practice.

Your practice, should contain the three essential elements:

1. Clear: Remove all that does not serve our greatest good from the energetic body.

2. Cultivate: Replenish energetic reserves, increase energy levels and invite restorative energy from external pure sources.

3. Connect: Experience moments of inner peace that provide clarity and affirmation for your work.

8. No Minimum Obligation Connected Check-Ins

1. Naps

2. Nature

3. No, I don't want to.

4. Music

5. Make

6. Move

7. Offline

8. Oasis

9. Oxygen

9. Conducting an Organizational Reading

1. Bubble: Prepare and protect your energy.

2. Interact: Move around the space intentionally and intuitively. Have an initial plan, but remain fluid.

3. Observe: Remain tuned to your senses with heightened curiosity.

4. Log Observations: Immediately log all that you observe.

5. Identify Insights: Begin by discovering which observations are connected.

6. Action: Identify where you should begin your work or what work is most pressing.

10. Designing a Team Intervention

Analysis

1. Conduct an organizational reading focused strictly on the team's stakeholders and environment.

2. Identify the team's active developmental phase.

Design

3. Identify objectives for the team intervention based on your analysis findings.

4. Write each objective as a SMART goal.

Develop

5. Create the sequence of activities that will be used to achieve identified objectives.

Implement

6. Facilitate Team Intervention.

Evaluate

7. Log observations and insights from team intervention.

8. Revisit log to identify future action items for team development.

11. Power Resume Design

Objective: Write a resume that aligns with your Connected Path.

Identify your personal skill sets that need to be highlighted in the resume.

1. Do this using the intuitive card deck of your preference. Setting the intention for your personal powers for this work to be revealed as you select 3 to 5 cards. If you need further guidance on facilitating the process of using the cards, please reference Chapter 17: Cards of Intuition in my previous book, The HR Intuitive.

Add the Revealed Personal Powers to your Resume.

2. After your contact information, create a section titled Relevant Skills. This resume will emphasize your skills before your work history.

3. Identify three of your revealed personal powers that are most relevant to the positions you will be applying for.

4. List each skill and underneath each one provide 3-5 points that prove that skill. These points provide a prospective employer with context of how these skills have materialized in the past and should include specific examples of work you have done.

5.   After the Relevant Skills section, provide a section for work history. You only need to list the names of the companies you worked for, with your job title and employment dates; specific responsibilities or duties are not necessary since they are highlighted in the skills section.

6. After Work History, list your relevant educational background as well as highlight any professional accomplishments or community engagement.

Note: This resume design is intended to attract prospective employers that will align with your Connected Path and utilize your skills and full capacity. It is not intended to increase appeal to the masses. Therefore, every rejection should be accepted as a blessing, since it is likely that organization would not be a workplace that would support your work.

12. Inner Purpose Meditation

Objective: Explore the messiness of life through a perspective of purpose to emerge with greater clarity.

1. Begin Natural Breathing.

2. Imagine yourself as a slow moving caterpillar inching along on a log. Take notice of the vivid details of the big world that surrounds you. You feel small and average, questioning what you have to offer. Your self-doubt gives you the munchies, so you pause to snack on a nearby berry.

3. Instead of allowing the gravity of doubt to pull you downward, use the energy to pull you inward. Withdraw - wrapping yourself in a warm cocoon.

4. Here in this safe space you can be your authentic self, allowing the messiness from within to ooze out in all directions fully exposed. As you watch what appears to be meaningless moments in life begin to merge, you take notice in the momentum they produce.

5. The messiness begins to give life to a substance that you were previously not aware of, one that warms the heart and feeds the soul.

6. This growth begins to amass becoming tangible like a protective shield of courage beginning to encompass your entire body.

7. As it begins to take shape, ask your inner self. "Why am I here? How am I meant to serve?"

8. Listen as your response is delivered in your unique Connected language, that only you understand.

9. When ready, begin to unravel yourself from the cocoon, and begin waking up the body slowly.

10. You should emerge from the cocoon with a bit more clarity of your purpose. Each time that you visit this cocoon of contemplation you will gain more courage, confidence and clarity until you are ready to fully expand your wings.

CHAPTER FIFTEEN

TOOLS TO HEAL THE MIND
by Bobbi Billman

A Director of Human Resources for a local school district, Bobbi spends her free time on her passion and purpose – helping others through yoga, meditation, and coaching. She is a 200 hour E-RYT and 500 hour RYT certified yoga teacher specializing in Gentle Hatha yoga, Yin yoga, Restorative yoga, and Chair yoga. She is also a 200-hour certified meditation teacher, a Reiki practitioner, a certified Nutrition coach, and a certified Life coach. She offers all these services through her yoga/wellness business, Ignite Yoga and Wellness. Her goal is to help individuals experience the many benefits of yoga, meditation, and good nutrition in order to heal their bodies and minds and live their best life, one small step at a time.

Inside this chapter you will find:

1. Inner Purpose Mediation
2. Fitting in Your Practice
3. Meditation for Reflection
4. Meditation for Slowing Down
5. The Significance of Breath
6. The 3-Part Breath
7. The Five Finger Breath
8. Square Breathing

9. Using Focus to Quiet the Mind

10. Two Minute Transitions

11. Giving Yourself Permission

12. How to Ground Yourself Quickly

You can find Bobbi online at Ignite Yoga & Wellness (www.myigniteyoga.com), Facebook (@MyIgniteYoga), and Instagram (@igniteyogayork).

1. Fitting in Your Practice

Objective: Fit meditation into your daily schedule.

There are many benefits to having a daily meditation practice. From decreased stress and anxiety to improved sleep and mood, we know meditation is good for us. The problem comes when we try to fit it into our hectic lives. Many people say they simply don't have time to meditate every day.

But the truth is you have to make time, otherwise the quality of your life, and the lives of those with whom you interact with daily, will suffer. While it can feel like there is never enough time for meditation, there are actually many ways to sneak a little meditation into your daily schedule.

Here are a few tips for squeezing meditation into your day:

1. Wake up 5-10 minutes earlier. Get it done before the craziness of the day begins. This allows you to get centered and focused for your day.

2. During your lunch break, while your food is heating up or right after you finish eating, take just a few minutes if only to breathe.

3. Right after work, in the car/garage before going in your house or as soon as you walk in the house (if no one is there to distract you).

4. Schedule it, just like any other appointment or meeting.

5. Micro-doses (take one minute, 5 or 10 times a day)

    a. Right when you wake up

    b. When you park your car at work (before going in)

    c. Between meetings

    d. Before or after lunch

    e. Before dinner

    f. Before bed

    g. Anytime you feel stressed

Don't make it harder than it has to be. A few simple minutes of quiet goes a long way on your meditation journey. Don't wait for perfect conditions. Make time today for a few minutes of meditation.

2. Meditation for Reflection

Objective: Use meditation to help you reflect.

There are many ways to pause and to reflect. Meditation is one of them. And truly it is one of my personal favorites.

But there are many misconceptions of meditation, which often prevent people from even giving it a try. At its core, meditation is all about pausing. Stopping and breathing. Being in the moment. And while we try to minimize our thoughts during meditation, it is not about stopping all thoughts from occurring. The quieting or slowing down of the mind, is the goal – not the ceasing of all thoughts. It is when the mind becomes more quiet that we can experience a period of reflection during our meditation.

So, let's take a moment for a very simple meditation. Find a quiet place to sit, somewhere you won't be disturbed. Sit comfortably in an upright position, with hands resting in your lap. Gently close your eyes and allow your breath to flow naturally. Relax your shoulders, your jaw, your fingers and toes. Feel your belly rise and fall with the breath.

Spend a few minutes with the breath – breathing in for a count of four, pausing at the top of the inhale for one second, then exhaling for a count of four and pausing at the end of the exhale for one second. Repeat this for two to three minutes. (No need to set a timer for this, just complete this breath pattern for about 12-15 rounds or until it feels complete for you.) Allow your body to relax into the breath. If you lose count of your inhales or exhales, simply start again on your next inhale.

Then allow your breath to go back to its normal, natural rhythm. Sit with the breath, allowing thoughts to come and go as they may, coming back to the focus on the breath when you notice it has drifted. You can sit for 5 minutes or more – it is up to you. Personally, I like sitting for 15-20 minutes, but find what works for you. Notice as you are sitting with your breath what comes up for you. What reflections creep in? We want to be careful to let them, like all thoughts, come and go in our meditation. We don't want to dwell on them. We simply notice them and go back to the breath.

After the meditation is over, take some time to notice those things that came up for you. Allow for a few minutes to reflect on your meditation. You can even journal in order to capture your reflections on paper before continuing with your day.

3. Meditation for Slowing Down

Objective: Use meditation to slow down the mind.

There are many wonderful benefits to meditation, but perhaps the biggest one is the fact that by its very nature it causes you to sit still and breathe which by default helps you to slow down. So, I invite you to take a few minutes to enjoy the meditation practice below, giving your body the opportunity to slow down and relax. So, let's get started…

Settle into a comfortable seat. Relax your shoulders down and away from your ears. Take a deep breath in and sigh it out. Come into your breath and into your body, allowing your muscles to relax a little bit more with each exhale.

Relax the crown of your head. Smooth out your forehead and soften the temples. Softly close your eyes if that is comfortable for you. Relax your cheeks and ears. Loosen your jaw and soften your throat. Let your arms be heavy, resting in your lap. Soften the elbows and relax your fingers. Relax your hips and buttocks. Soften your knees and relax your toes. Feel the heaviness of the body as your muscles relax.

Now turn your focus to your breath. Follow each inhale and each exhale, feeling the breath at the tip of the nostrils. Feel the coolness of the inhale and the warmth of the exhale. Continue to allow the body to relax into the breath. Let go of your day. Let go of any stresses or tensions you are holding on to at this moment. Just try to be here in your body with the breath, releasing everything else for just a few minutes.

Let's begin to control the breath a bit more now, inhaling for a count of four, holding at the top of the inhale for one second, releasing the breath for a count of four, then hold the breath at the end of the exhale for one second. Continue breathing in this way for a few moments, allowing thoughts to come and go as they may. Just keep the focus on the breath. (Ideally 2-4 minutes if possible, but you can always work up to this.)

Then release the control of the breath, allowing your breathing to go back to its normal, natural pace. Feel the breath move in your body. Feel your body connected to the ground beneath you, allowing your body and mind to slowly transition back to the present moment.

Begin to gently wiggle your fingers and toes. Rock your head softly from side to side. Take a deep breath in as you reach your arms up overhead, then sigh it out as you release the arms back down. And then when you are feeling ready, slowly open your eyes.

4. The Significance of Breath

Objective: Breathe to heal.

The Natural Breath, called such because it happens naturally. Organically. Without effort. It flows in and out without a need on our part to direct or control it. We can be thankful this is how it works, otherwise some of us might be in serious trouble. ☺ But in all seriousness, the natural breath is truly a blessing. But not just because it happens automatically. It is also a blessing, albeit in a slightly different way, when we take control of it as well. You see, breathing isn't just essential to living, though that is obviously important. It is also essential to our overall health and wellbeing.

Bold words. How so, you may ask. Let's take a moment to revisit an age-old story. When we feel threatened or stressed in any way, our bodies will enter into one of three responses – fight, flight, or freeze. What we mean by this is that our body, including our breath, changes in a way to support our selected response (fight, flight, or freeze) to the stressor we are facing in an attempt to successfully overcome the stressor.

It is important to understand that our body doesn't know the difference between an actual physical stressor versus a perceived stressor. In other words, your body will respond the same if a lion is right in front of you about to pounce and eat you as it will if you are afraid of failing a major test or of not getting that big promotion to better support your family. A stressor is a stressor is a stressor, at least as far as the impact of the stress on your body and mind are concerned.

So regardless of the stressor, your body will respond in the same fight, flight, or freeze way. This is important to know as it helps you come to terms with the power of the mind to suggest or control your reality. But understanding what is happening and why it is happening is only part of the puzzle. We also have to figure out what to do to bring our bodies and minds back from that stressed place, to release the accumulated stress from the situation.

In the wild when animals are stressed (picture a gazelle being chased by a lion), they also experience the fight, flight, or freeze response in their bodies just as we do. What's remarkably different though is how they come out of that stressed state (assuming they have successfully evaded their stressor). Our gazelle, for example, once the lion is gone (the stressor is physically no longer present), will shake almost uncontrollably. It is fascinating to watch (just pull up any wildlife documentary and watch how an animal shakes after the stressor is gone). This is their body literally shaking off the stress of that precious moment to release it.

Humans on the other hand do not shake like that when their stressor is gone. Perhaps we should, but we do not. Maybe we give a sigh of relief, take a bubble bath, get a massage, go to the gym, have an adult beverage, or eat a pint of ice cream, but we don't physically shake off the stress of our experience. And, spoiler alert, all those examples of things I just listed that we do for ourselves as either a reward or an attempt at post-stress self-care *do not* release the stress. They may temporarily make us feel a little better, but the stress of the experience is still in our body, held by our organs and muscles.

Okay, so as humans we tend to hold on to our stress. But it was just one stressful situation, so what's the big deal? When was the last time you only had one stress response in a day? Likely never. The reality of the society in which we all live today is such that we are almost always in high stress mode, moving from one stressor to another, which is terribly problematic. If we can't come out of that stress mode and allow our bodies time to rest, relax, and fully release the stress from our multitudes of stressors, our bodies never get a break. It's like continually revving the engine of your car even when it is in park. Over time that continual accumulation of stress held in the body leads to all kinds of issues, including diseases.

For now, let's focus on what we can do about it. How can we break that stress cycle, or in other words, how can we "shake off" our stress? And with that we are now full circle – back to the natural breath.

Learning to control the breath in certain ways helps the body to transition from that stressed state (when the sympathetic nervous system is calling all the shots) to a calmer, more relaxed state (when the parasympathetic system kicks in and begins to release the stress collected in the body). There are many breathing techniques out there. For our purposes we will stick to a few of the basic ones.

Included are three breathing techniques that will help your body shift out of that stressed state.

Keep in mind as we go through these breathing techniques, that they may not all resonate with you and that's okay. Try them. See which one(s) work best for you and remember that all new things take time. Practice is key. Stick with it and you will begin to see major shifts in how you manage your stress. Come back to these anytime you need them.

Breath is a vital part of living. And it is a superpower against stress when we use it in the right ways. The good news is that it isn't hard to do any of these breathing techniques. Play with them, practice them, and find what works for you. Help your body let go of stress, the tightness, and the tension we hold in our bodies which lead to so many other unfortunate ailments.

5. The 3-Part Breath

Objective: Release stress in your body through controlled breathing.

For this breathing technique you will want to sit or stand comfortably, making sure your posture is tall, providing plenty of room for the torso to expand as you breathe. Eyes closed is an option if that feels appropriate to you, otherwise keep them open.

This breath is a slow and controlled breath in which we take a deep inhale filling the torso from the belly up into the rib cage area and then into the chest area. At the top of the inhale, we pause for a second before allowing for a slow controlled exhale, releasing the breath first from the chest, then the rib cage area, and finally from the belly. Then pause at the bottom of the exhale for a second before repeating the breath again.

You can do this breath for as long as you want, but usually, when releasing stress is the focus, it is best to breathe in this way for at least two minutes if you can. Remember that doing the breath even for 30 seconds is better than not doing it at all, but if you can give it at least two minutes, please do.

The beauty of this breath is that you can do it anywhere. You can be driving (eyes open please), in a meeting, watching TV, sitting quietly… you get the idea. You can easily insert it into your day as you go from one activity to another. Just imagine how you would feel if you practiced this breathing technique in between every meeting and as you transitioned between work and home. Think of the amount of stress you could release if you made it a part of your daily routines.

Additional tip: Try placing one hand on your belly and one on your heart when doing this breath to help you to really connect with or feel the breath, further helping you to calm the body as you breathe.

6. The Five-Finger Breath

Objective: Release stress in your body through controlled breathing.

While sitting or standing comfortably, lay one of your hands on a flat surface, like a desk or table. Spread your fingers out wide. Using the index finger of your other hand, trace up the outside of your thumb (of the hand laying on the flat surface) while inhaling. Pause for a second at the top of the thumb, then trace down the inside of that thumb while exhaling. Pause at the base of the thumb. Allow your tracing movement to follow the speed of your breath, linking your movement to the breath. Next, inhale and trace up the index finger of that hand, pausing for a second at the top of that finger. Then exhale and trace down the other side of that index finger, pausing at the base of the finger for a second. Do this for the other three fingers as well, then repeat it going back the other direction (from the pinky finger to the thumb). You can trace your five fingers as many times as you would like, even switching hands if you want. Try to aim for at least two minutes with this breathing practice if you can.

Additional tip: This is a great breathing exercise for someone who is a tactile learner (likes to use their hands or touch things when they engage with them). Another option, especially good for children, is to use a pencil or crayon to trace the fingers on paper while breathing.

7. Square Breathing

Objective: Release stress in your body through controlled breathing.

For this breath we will be drawing a square as we breathe so it can be done on a flat surface like the previous breath technique or you can draw the square in "mid-air" or in your mind. This breath can be done seated or standing, with eyes open or closed, whichever options feel best to you.

On your inhale use one of your index fingers to draw a line in an upward direction, then pause for one second. On your exhale, use that finger to draw a line across and to the right, pausing at the end of the exhale. Next, inhale while drawing the line straight down, pausing at the end of the inhale. Then draw a line across and to the left (back to our starting point) on the exhale. Pause again for a second at the end of the exhale. Allow your movement to follow the speed of your breath, linking your movement to the breath. You can repeat this as often as you want, but as always, try to aim for at least two minutes.

Additional tip: This is another great breathing exercise for someone who is a tactile learner (likes to use their hands or touch things when they engage with them). Again, you can also use a pencil or crayon to trace the square on paper while breathing if you prefer.

8. Using Focus to Quiet the Mind

Objective: An alternative method to Quiet the Monkey Mind.

Quieting the mind. Mindfulness. Meditating. Many of us are familiar with these concepts, but despite our familiarity with them, they often feel unattainable.

There's little arguing the fact that we live in a fast-paced society filled with constant stimuli. There's so much to process and so many distractions. It is hard to quiet the mind in that kind of environment which negatively impacts our sleep and our overall focus.

Many people have a false notion that quieting the mind, meditating, and mindfulness require the complete emptying of the mind, however this is not usually the case. Ultimately this may be the goal for some meditators, but for most of us quieting the mind is about calming the mind and slowly eliminating the distractors in order to be able to focus, think more clearly, or reduce stress.

That constant chatter in our minds is often referred to as monkey mind. If the term monkey mind doesn't resonate with you, perhaps the term unfocused mind is better suited. If you are a visual person, try visualizing the image of a highly caffeinated hamster running on his little wheel inside your head. Regardless of what you wish to call it or how you want to picture it, you get the general idea – there's constant chatter or noise inside our heads. 24/7/365. This can easily add to stress, preventing us from being productive at work, attentive to relationships, and more...

So how do we dial all that noise down a notch or two? Let's look at some things we can do to help rein in all that mental chatter.

When practicing a balance pose in yoga, instructors will have you find a *dristi*, a gaze or focal point, to help you hold the pose successfully. When we are attempting to quiet the mind a dristi is equally as helpful. A variety of items can serve this purpose. Here are a few examples:

Breath Work: Without a doubt, breath work can help with quieting the mind. There are so many different breathwork techniques that can help with this. For a few specific breath work tips and techniques check out the previous sections.

Mantra: Another great way to quiet the mind is to focus on a mantra. Traditionally said mentally in Sanskrit (the ancient language of India), mantras are words or sounds repeated to help you focus your mind. These can be inspirational, motivational, or spiritual in nature. You silently say the mantra in conjunction with the breath. One of the most common mantras is *So Hum* – you mentally say So on the inhale, then Hum as you exhale. Just as following the breath helps us pin down our mental focus, mentally repeating a mantra can help us let go of other distracting thoughts.

Candle or Object: Simply having something to stare out, to focus on, can help you to quiet your mind. Watching the flicker of a candle flame or the flames of a fire are excellent examples. But truthfully, any stationary object that you can look at without it causing additional thoughts to come up for you, will work. Some other examples could be a spot on the floor, a wall, or a door. You could even stare out a window at something off in the distance. Truthfully what the object is that you are staring at does not matter if it allows you to focus and begin to release some of that mental chatter.

9. Two-Minute Transitions

Objective: Successfully transitioning throughout your day.

Many of us rush through our days from one activity to another. Meeting after meeting. Class after class. Work in the office followed by work at home. Running around all day at work and then running around all evening with the kids. We barely have time to breathe, let allow process our day. Sound familiar? It is all too common and is largely the cause of the chronic stress epidemic in the United States.

One way to combat this, as well as help to quiet the mind, is implementing the use of two-minute transitions. The idea of pausing for two minutes (or less if you can't spare two minutes) to breathe and let go of whatever you are coming from before going on to what is next.

So, what does this look like? Well, it could be deep breathing walking down the hall from one meeting to the next. It could be closing your office door or retreating to the restroom so you can close your eyes, do a few stretches, or even silently let out your frustrations. It might be sitting in your car an extra two minutes before going into work at the start of your day or into your house at the end of the day. You get the idea. There are limitless options for how you can use two-minute transitions.

Again, whether it ends up being 20 seconds or two minutes, the net result is you and your body have a chance to decompress from one stressful, hectic event before heading into another. This is a fabulous tool for both quieting the mind and processing your emotions. It will allow you to go into your next meeting or activity with a clearer focus, a calmer demeanor, and a quieter mind.

10. Giving Yourself Permission

Objective: Accepting your practice however it presents itself on any given day.

Another important part of learning to quiet your mind is to give yourself permission. Permission to miss a day of your meditation or breathing practice. Permission to not stay focused during a practice. In other words, permission to be human. Anyone who has meditated, done mindfulness work, and/or tried to quiet the mind has had days when their practice felt really good or successful as well as days when they could barely stop the mental chatter at all thus making them feel like a failure at this practice. Both are normal, even for long time practitioners. Give yourself permission to have whatever kind of practice you are meant to have at that moment. And then endeavor to give it a try again tomorrow.

If you have attempted to meditate, quiet your mind, or complete a mindfulness activity, then you likely know that the mental chatter doesn't go away easily. That is why quieting the mind is a practice. Just like learning a new skill in basketball or learning to play a new instrument, it takes time, patience, and practice.

Over time you will notice the chatter decreases, not only when you are trying to quiet the mind through one of these techniques, but also throughout your day in general. In other words, it can become a habit. It is important to have patience and to keep practicing. Be observant. Notice what time of day is better for you to practice quieting your mind and which techniques work better for you, and then capitalize on them.

11. How to Ground Yourself Quickly

Objective: Healing through a quick grounding technique.

Grounding is a term that might be new to you, though it has slowly become a part of the common vernacular over the past few years. Grounding, sometimes referred to as earthing, is simply connecting to the ground, or the earth, beneath your feet. It's simple and free, and anyone can do it.

Ideally you would be outside on the grass, the dirt, or the sand in your bare feet allowing for a direct connection between you and the Earth. When you do, you are literally connecting to the energies of the Earth. The Earth has a negative charge, but humans have a positive charge, so when we come in contact with the Earth, we exchange energies, giving off some of our positive charge and picking up some of the Earth's negative charge.

Scientifically speaking, it has been shown that this simple practice provides numerous benefits including boosting your immunity, reducing stress, and improving sleep. It also helps you to feel more balanced, centered, and focused.

The fastest and easiest way to ground yourself is to take off your shoes and stand (or walk) barefoot on the grass, dirt, or sand. Try to spend at least 5 minutes connecting directly to the earth. If you are standing still, you can close your eyes and relax into a breathing technique of your choice. If you go for a walk, focus on the earth beneath your bare feet, feeling that connection with each step.

If going outside is not an option for you due to your schedule or the weather, you can also look into grounding products such as earthing mats, bed pads, chairs, or body bands. Those can be easy substitutes if getting out into nature is not an option for you.

No matter which method you choose, grounding is one of the easiest and most powerful tools for bringing healing into your body.

CHAPTER SIXTEEN

TOOLS FOR ADDITIONAL SUPPORT
by Kimberly Preske, MSW, LSW

Kimberly Preske provides outpatient therapy in Hanover, Pennsylvania. She uses her personal and professional experiences to teach about school shooting and community trauma pre-education and recovery. The State University of New York College of Environmental Science and Forestry trained her to be a critical thinker. Becoming a Temple University educated social worker opened her eyes to the challenges faced and overcome by so many amazing individuals. Presentation inquiries can be sent to Kimberly.preske@gmail.com.

Inside this chapter you will find:

1. Suicide

2. Crisis

3. Employee Assistance Programs

4. Types of Mental Health Providers

5. Finding and Paying for your Mental Health Provider

6. Substance Use Treatments

7. Building a Support Team

8. Why Would Someone See a Mental Health Professional?

9. How Long Do People Work with a Therapist?

10. Being in the Present

1. Suicide

If you or someone you know is having a mental health emergency, please call 911 or The National Suicide Prevention Lifeline at 800-273-TALK (8255) immediately.

Hope and help are available. There are people who can understand how you feel, listen, and provide support.

People can experience a wide range of experiences within suicidality. When I was experiencing suicidal feelings and thoughts, I felt very alone and simply wanted the pain to end. I did not want to die and could name all the things that I would miss in the future. At the same time, I could not figure out a way to reduce the pain on my own. Oddly it sounded very logical in my own head that suicide was an option. I am so grateful that I connected with people who understood and could listen to what I was feeling and thinking.

2. Crisis

A crisis may be more than thoughts of suicide. A crisis can be that a person's coping skills are overwhelmed. There are many crisis lines that can be called 24 hours a day, seven days a week. Including but not limited to crisis lines for mental health, domestic violence, disasters and veterans.

I encourage people to call a crisis line to learn what it is like before they or a family member experience a crisis. Calling a crisis or suicide prevention number does not mean that automatically lights and sirens will immediately be sent to your home. This is a common misconception that can keep people from calling.

Crisis lines are staffed by trained, supportive people who are often available at the most lonely and vulnerable times like in the middle of the night or on holidays. Often people call crisis lines so they can talk with someone when their friends and family are unavailable. Being connected can make a huge difference.

Most communities have local crisis lines. In the United States there is a national crisis text line that you can text "Home" to 741741 to connect with a crisis counselor.

NAMI National Alliance on Mental Illness (NAMI) helpline at 800-950-NAMI is also available in the United States. Many states have local NAMI chapters that offer free peer led support groups for people who are experiencing mental health concerns. NAMI also offers free classes and support groups for family and friends.

Many states in the United States offer a service where you can dial 211 on your phone. 211 can provide many local referrals for many essential services beyond mental health. Some 211 sites also offer trained compassionate listeners.

If you are experiencing a crisis, you may be surprised how helpful it is to talk with a kind, compassionate person.

3. Employee Assistance Programs

Employee Assistance Program (EAP) benefits are often underutilized. EAP services are provided by some employers as an additional benefit separate from medical insurance. If your employer offers EAP services, they can connect you with the EAP company who contracts with a network of mental health providers. You typically do not need to opt in to enroll in EAP benefits from your employer.

The EAP company connects employees with a mental health provider for a limited number of free sessions. Typically, 3-10 sessions may be provided free of charge per program year, per issue or one time only. Frequently EAP sessions are also available to the employees' family members and even other people who live in their homes. These sessions can be used for a wide variety of reasons including family conflict, work challenges, mental health symptoms and more. It can be helpful to ask to be connected to a provider who accepts your insurance if you need to continue treatment beyond the free sessions.

Sometimes employees do not use their EAP benefits because they think their employer will know that they are using the EAP services or will know what they discuss. Employees have confidentiality while seeing an EAP mental health provider most of the time just as they would when seeing someone using their insurance. Typically, the only time employers are told employees are seeing an EAP mental health provider is if the employee is required or mandated to see an EAP provider as a condition of their continued employment. Examples for a mandated referral may be work attendance, performance issues or conflicts in the workplace. If an employer mandates an employee to see a mental health provider, the employee would need to complete a release of information for any information to be released to their employer.

4. Types of Mental Health Providers

When you begin to look for a mental health professional, you may notice there are many different options.

Are you looking for a therapist, a clinician or a counselor?

Would you prefer to see a clinical social worker, a Licensed Professional Counselor or a psychologist?

How about a pastoral counselor who provides counseling in a faith-based setting?

Maybe you are seeking help in your family or marriage relationships and would like to connect with a Licensed Marriage Family Therapist.

If you are looking for psychiatric medication management, would you prefer to see a psychiatrist or a psychiatric or mental health nurse practitioner?

Each of these professionals has a different educational background, credentials, and ways of providing support and treatment. You may want to spend a little time researching the differences and deciding what feels right for you.

The National Alliance on Mental Illness (NAMI) webpage "Types of Mental Health Providers" may be helpful in exploring what type of mental health provider you may wish to see.

https://www.nami.org/About-Mental-Illness/Treatments/Types-of-Mental-Health-Professionals

It can also help to ask people you trust who they may recommend.

5. Finding and Paying for a Mental Health Provider

If you would like to use your insurance, the most direct way to find a provider is to call the member number on the back of your insurance card. Ask for the names and phone numbers for mental health providers who accept your insurance in the area you are looking for. You can tell the insurance company what symptoms or experiences you are looking for help with. To understand your benefits, you will ask for the following benefits:

Deductible: an amount that you pay out of pocket before the insurance company begins to pay a portion of what is owed to providers. You may have an individual and/or family deductible. Sometimes there are separate deductibles for different types of services.

Copay: a set amount you pay for a visit or a medication each time.

Coinsurance: a percentage of the cost you pay after your deductible is met.

Explanation of benefits (EOB): a statement of how your insurance company processed a provider claim. EOBs are often mailed or can be viewed in your insurance company's member portal.

When you call individual provider offices, you can ask to speak for 15 minutes with a mental health provider to decide if they would be a good match for you.

If you find a provider who is not in-network with your insurance that you would really like to work with, you can ask if they are willing to submit for out-of-network benefits to your insurance company. Then you can call your insurance provider to ask what your out-of-network benefits are (out-of-network deductible, copay, coinsurance). You can also ask the provider if they offer a sliding scale rate for paying out-of-pocket (also known as a cash rate). They may also offer lower cost (a sliding scale) or pro bono sessions if you have financial challenges that you can apply for.

6. Substance Use Treatments

In some states and countries, mental health and substance use can be treated by the same provider. In other places, there may be requirements for certain types of providers with specific training and certifications.

Peer support can be a helpful part of substance use recovery for individuals and their family members. Alcoholics Anonymous (AA) and Al-Anon/alateen family groups provide support for many people. Any meetings that are labeled as open are available for anyone to attend. Other specific meetings are labeled and explained on meeting calendars. Narcotics Anonymous (NA) and Nar-Anon are also available in many areas. Because NA meetings may not be offered as frequently as AA meetings, many people attend AA meetings as well. Smart Recovery and the faith-based Celebrate Recovery may be a great fit as well. Be open to checking out several meetings as each setting may be different.

Certified recovery specialists are individuals who have lived experience and training to be a role model, advocate, and mentor. Their transparency about their personal experiences and knowledge about systems and services makes them a valuable member of a recovery team.

7. Building a Support Team

Building a team approach can be helpful in that it provides support across a person's life in all areas. Working with a therapist or counselor is a specific type of relationship within boundaries and limits. Family and friends are natural supports. Group support like peer-based groups validate how people are feeling and can connect people to additional experiences and tools that may be helpful.

Medical professionals including primary care doctors (family doctors), dentists, gynecologists, and other specialists can help with ruling out medical causes, treating symptoms, and prescribing medications. Holistic providers and practices like acupuncture, massage, medical qigong, tai chi, and yoga can teach relaxation, help create safety in the body, and provide ways for the body to release the internalized stress and trauma.

8. Why Would Someone See a Mental Health Professional?

There are many times when seeking the help of a mental health professional may be beneficial. This is far from an inclusive list.

When you need an unbiased person who can listen and reflect things back to you

Having support may be helpful:

- To learn skills to make a change
- If you are having difficulty with relationships
- To process experiences in school or at work
- Having symptoms that are not explained by a physical health diagnosis
- If you experience a crisis, trauma, death, or disaster and need a safe place to talk, process or be heard
- Have trouble functioning like getting to or being at school or work, completing daily tasks to meet your basic needs or those of your family members

- Are impacted by substance use

- Have difficulty managing emotions, feel lonely, disconnected, or are not interested in activities that used to make you happy

- Experience flashbacks or intrusions from experiences you have had

- Have challenges with eating

- Are sleeping too much or too little. Or having trouble falling asleep or staying asleep.

9. How Long Do People Work with a Therapist?

Everyone is different, because they have their own personal reasons for seeing a therapist. At the first appointment (intake), you and the mental health professional will discuss what you are experiencing, want to explore, change and/or learn. Then the two of you will talk about setting goals, how frequently you will meet and make a plan to accomplish your goals.

Some people meet a therapist for only a few Employee Assistance Program provided sessions for a specific challenge or situation. Others may work with a therapist for many years. Some individuals see someone for a while, then take a break and return months or years later.

I often look at therapy like a rest stop where people may focus on refueling themselves, create a toolbox of skills, and have a safe place to share their experiences, hopes and dreams. They take what happens in the office out into their world to be empowered to create the life they want.

10. Being in the Present

Sometimes people become unable to be in the present because their emotions, thoughts, and physical reactions are overwhelming. Being able to slow down, take a pause, and become centered in the present again can help bring you back into the here and now.

I like being connected to things around me physically. You can stomp your feet and root them into the floor. Push up against a wall or into a corner. Hold an object in your hand like a heavy bracelet, full ring of keys, or a smooth stone.

Sometimes changing where you are or what you are doing can disrupt the feelings or thoughts. Go for a walk, or open a window and get some fresh air. Have someone take you for a drive and feel the sun, rain, or wind on your face. Take a cool drink of water or stand in front of the open refrigerator. Hold a glass of water with ice in your hands, feeling the cool moisture dripping in your hands. Slow your breathing and focus on each inhale and exhale.

Look around you and start describing something that is present. You can say it out loud, think it silently in your head, write or draw it out. Call a friend or family member or tell a safe person who may be nearby. Get detailed. What are you seeing? How would you describe the shades of colors? Are all the colors of the rainbow around you? What shapes do you see? Explore the size and compare it to other things nearby. Are you able to touch it? How does it feel? Have you noticed it before? Do you smell anything in the air or room you are in? Can you hear anything? Is there a happy or funny memory that you can think of that may relate to what you are observing? Would you want to own it? Does it fit the personality of someone else you know? Be curious like a scientist and explore your environment like it is the first time you have ever been there.

As you become more and more detailed, and with some practice, you may find that the overwhelming thoughts and feelings quiet the mind as you are able to focus on what is in front of you. Breathe one breath, one second, one moment at a time.

11. Trauma

In 2003, I was impacted by a community-based trauma, its aftermath and recovery. Although I was the first adult to be seen and sought help twice more in the first thirty-four hours, I was not given a direct referral to mental health services. Years later I connected to a spiritual director who was able to listen and witness my pain.

Then I spent time with a survivor of another school incident who normalized my experience through sharing her own story. She was able to set boundaries and limits about what she could offer. Then she connected me to a responder who provided a referral to a therapist that was a certified trauma specialist. I had lived with untreated Post Traumatic Stress Disorder (PTSD) for 5 years before I began treatment with a therapist.

Everyone experiences trauma differently. Each person processes in their own way and on their own timeline. Sometimes people are recovering in ways that may feel harmful or painful to other people because we each have our own perspective and needs.

Your experiences, thoughts, and feelings are yours. You can advocate for what you need, and do not need to justify it to anyone else. I felt like I was less than and did not deserve help because of my role, job, and other people's reactions. That kept me from getting help sooner.

Group support from other people who are doing well in their own recovery can help connect individuals to find services and support. Having your experiences normalized by other people can reduce feeling isolated and alone. Trauma often has pieces of grief interconnected, and being seen, heard, and validated provides opportunities to share in a safe place.

Trauma is an emotional reaction to a disturbing event usually where the person feels unsafe. Events like community traumas, childhood trauma, and cumulative stress from repeated exposure to disturbing events or experiences can all change a person's perspective of themselves, others, and their environment. Making an appointment with a mental health professional can help explore the events you have experienced and how they may be impacting you.

12. Developing a Therapeutic Relationship

At times it can take calling or meeting several therapists to find one to begin working with. A therapeutic fit is when both a therapist's and a client's experience and knowledge allow for developing goals and working together within specific limits and boundaries. Training, style, personality, availability, and pacing all contribute to creating a safe space to experiment and learn in. Sometimes a therapist will recognize that they are not the best equipped, trained, or may have a conflict of interest that requires the therapist to refer the client to another provider. Regardless, it is important to recognize that this is a relationship and finding the best fit is essential for it to be successful. Please do not give up on seeking support because the first provider wasn't a great fit. All providers are different and your provider is out there ready to help.

ACKNOWLEDGMENTS

I must start this gratitude practice by recognizing the one individual that made all this possible—Demi Stevens, my editor and writing coach. Demi, you worked your magic to release this intuitive writing voice, and for that I will be forever grateful. Writing as a practice has changed my life. Your nudges are priceless and have been powerful guideposts when I needed it most to push through the inner critic attempting to sabotage this book.

My soul sister, Bobbi Billman, not only did you gift your words for the foreword and toolkit of this book, but you've always been with me every step of this journey. You've listened to random thoughts for hours, perhaps days, as I was actively attempting to make sense of it all. You also gave me the love and support when I needed it most to keep moving forward when my ego was terrified of the unknown. Without you, my work wouldn't be where it is, and I wouldn't be who I am today.

Kim Preske, it's safe to say that you have impacted my life beyond words. You were my very first coaching client and honestly the only reason I began working with individuals in the first place. You pushed me to realize that I had more to offer than my complacent skillsets. This was the seed I needed planted to sprout my active growth journey—a journey that is bigger and wilder than anything I could have ever dreamed.

Steph Holmes, you were the missing puzzle piece I have been waiting for. Your unswaying belief in the work gives me strength when things are hard. I am grateful for your wisdom and insight.

Josh, Maddy and Zoey, your love and support while I dive into my writing coma is one of the greatest blessings. It is your unconditional love and acceptance that nourishes my soul at the deepest level and makes all this matter.

I would now like to shift this gratitude practice to focus on the group of people this book is dedicated to. In Fall 2021, I completed my Master's Certificate in Medical Qigong at the East Coast Institute of Medical Qigong in Gettysburg, Pennsylvania. It was this program that awakened me to my calling as a healer and it was my teacher and classmates that made that transformation beautiful.

Diane, you pushed me in ways you never knew. You served as a mirror filled with grace and compassion, gently reminding me of the work I desperately wanted to suppress and forget. Thank you for always pulling it to the surface in the most loving way.

Karen, from the first day in class you embraced me in the warmest energetic hold. Holding me in your loving light, you created the space for me to unwind and let me guard down. Because of you I came to class everyday, heart open and fearless, knowing without a doubt that you had me and would let no harm come my way.

Chuck, I think it's safe to say our friendship bewilders most people. Yet, in you I found a friend who brings me so much joy. At times I feel we are connected energetic siblings, having divine timing to reach out and care for the other when we can be of assistance. I am so grateful for you. You are my Herbal Medicine Man.

Gwen, our time together has offered some of my greatest treasures for this lifetime. With you it is so natural. I live for our conversations where we are lost in the random streams of consciousness inspired by life and connection. I love how we can explore and unpack common experiences, enlightening each other. Every time I'm with you I feel like my heart becomes more open and my soul dances with delight, beaming.

Lyle, there literally are no words for our friendship. Thinking of you coming into my life and what you mean to me moves me to tears… tears of deep gratitude and love. You are the first person I have encountered in this life who sees me. Sometimes, I think you see me when I can't see myself. You carry me when life is hard and sit with me when I am impatient. I am so grateful that God intertwined our paths.

Ted, you were the perfect teacher. I know if it wasn't for you, I wouldn't be a healer today. I am grateful for the small details that make your teaching so powerful. Your humor and playfulness made the space less scary and me more open. Your invitations to "simply try" allowed me to dip in and begin. Your feedback was always gentle enough to push me yet not shut me down. Thank you for being you and thank you for bringing this incredible modality into my life.

About the Author

Samm Smeltzer is an HR Visionary and Medical Qigong Healer. In November 2021, she earned her Master's certification in Medical Qigong with Ted O'Brien at the East Coast Institute of Medical Qigong. Her decade-long pursuit of missing elements for employee engagement within organizations led her down this path of merging Spirituality, Eastern Medicine, and workplace wellness to create the potential for deep healing within workplace cultures.

Samm is the founder of The HRart Center, devoted to corporate wellness and growth. As a Medical Qigong Therapist, Samm's clients come from a range of backgrounds, but she specializes in healing stress and burnout for professionals as well as coaching them back to their Connected Path. The HRart Center's ultimate mission is to train HR professionals to become HR healers so they can heal their own workplaces. This is the workplace revolution we need.

She is currently pursuing her doctoral certificate in Medical Qigong at the 3 Treasures School of Medical Qigong, studying under Lisa VanOstrand.

To learn more about Samm's work go to, www.HRartcenter.com.